THE SALES SECRET

THE SALES SECRET

A Journey Toward Effortless Sales Success

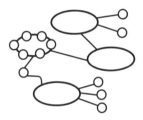

RICK DAVIS

Hard Knock Press

To book Rick as a speaker for your next event or to learn more about sales and sales management training programs for your company, visit **www.buildingleaders.com**

First published by Hard Knock Press, March 2012

Cover design by Lynda Van Duerm

ISBN: 978-0-9847114-0-6

Library of Congress Control Number: 2012934102

For Meg, my rock,
who believed in me
even when I was just
a salesman in a van
down by the river

Contents

Preface

I started writing this book many years ago. Then I stopped. Then I started. I wanted to craft a message but couldn't find the inspiration to author a book I believed worthy. The last thing I wanted to do was create another book on the "process" of selling that would read as dryly as so many I have studied in my career.

I eventually tossed months of work into the garbage when I deleted nine chapters and more than thirty thousand words. Instead of a "classroom" monologue, I decided to start anew by creating the characters of Adam and Abe from my own experiences. As you read the dialogue between Adam, the open-minded pupil, and Abe, his sagacious mentor, you will discover that it is a dialogue between us—you and me.

My goal in writing *The Sales Secret* was to touch the reader by addressing the psychological challenges of a very difficult profession. Selling, as Adam says, is a profession that always demands "more." The successes of past weeks and months are constantly replaced with a new set of quotas and goals. He struggles, like every salesperson, to overcome the incessant pressure he feels every day. Adam embarks on a journey to discover the secret of sales success by replacing the pressure with a process that will produce results and give him pride in his work.

The concept of the "sales secret" is a double entendre. The first secret defines the real process of making sales happen—that is, engaging in a non-linear process that flows according to real life, not some prescribed, unrealistic formula. On another level, the subtler secret is that success for salespeople should not be measured merely in their results. Success is based on the value that the sales professional brings to other people. These were the messages I aimed to convey in this book.

I additionally wanted to challenge the existing, but faulty, paradigms of sales that have been taught and re-taught for decades. Most of the frustration I experienced early in my sales career stemmed from the theoretical classroom lessons that provided impractical advice and, more importantly, stressed manipulation rather than cooperation. I have tried to bridge the gap between classroom theory and practical application in the real world by providing sales concepts that produce mutually beneficial relationships.

Finally, I wanted to introduce new concepts to the profession. I am not an advocate of the idea that there is nothing new to teach in the sales profession. I believe that we live in a world of complex emotions, technology, and sophisticated interaction. The methods that worked forty, or even fifteen, years ago are outdated. Adam's journey introduces him to concepts of Non-Linear Reality and Aikido, just a couple of the book's ideas that are not predominant among mainstream sales training classes. The sales profession is evolving and new ideas are not only emerging, they are essential.

My ultimate goal in this book was to reveal, not teach, what the sales process entails. During my two decades of lectures on the subject of selling, I find most veteran salespeople believe that my lessons bring out the ideas each of us already possess. The idea in this book is for every reader to find something personal in this story that helps convert experiences into learning lessons that produce sales success and confidence in the workplace and life.

The Sales Secret is written for every salesperson, manager, and business professional that has felt moments of stress while trying to convince others to take action. I hope you will realize that victory begins with a vision. You simply manifest that vision by changing your focus to contribute to the betterment of others. In the end, selling is about one simple lesson: Reduce your expectations for personal gain and increase your intentions to help others. From there, the results will come easily...

Acknowledgments

My wife, Meg, normally an intense editor of my words, after reviewing early chapters, said only five words, "This is it. Keep writing." That was the spark of inspiration I needed. The story and lessons flowed from there.

Craig Webb, Editor of *ProSales Magazine* and the writing mentor who has coached me for many years on the nuances of crafting a story, read the manuscript and generously guided me toward an efficiency of words. I owe it to him and my book shepherd, Suzanne Murray, along with Sarah McCarry, of StyleMatters for helping me produce a flow that (hopefully) engages the reader. Suzanne's advice was the instrumental finishing touch that ensured quality, flow, and character development.

This book was influenced daily by Ellice Herman, who literally read each chapter with me aloud and provided steady encouragement, practical insights, and instrumental edits while dealing with the difficult mood swings of an author struggling to finish the project. Ellice's wonderful contributions helped bring the book to life.

Two of my dear friends, Matt Berley and Mark Hansen (successful sales warriors both), told me I had captured the emotions that most salespeople feel. Yet, they each independently told me to take more risks and bring out the characters and settings in the story. Mike and Heidi Lopez are two dear friends that also guided me along the same path. Because of these friends, I was unblocked and freely tried to paint better pictures in words.

The golf instructor I mention in the book is really my piano teacher, Dr. Pawel Checinski, a Fulbright Scholar and Julliard Doctor of Musical Arts who is the best teacher I have ever known. He reminds me weekly what it means to be a good student and to focus on the small, effortless actions that eventually add up to big results.

I would be remiss if I did not mention Kathy Ziprik, the most talented and energetic PR Specialist I have ever known. For fifteen years, she graciously has given her time and expertise as communicator to enhance the content of my work and exposure of my message to thousands of readers.

The cover design and, for that matter, all my graphic design work, come from the hand of Lynda Van Duerm, whose artistry and professionalism never cease to amaze me. The layout of this book was created by two other members of the outstanding team at StyleMatters, Bonnie Bushman and Jerry Dorris. Their thoughts and creativity brought a wonderful texture to the story.

I literally could thank thousands of salespeople, mentors, and business leaders I have met on my journey, each of whom has shared their story and a lesson that contributes to my teaching and inspiration for the lessons in this book.

I lastly wish to acknowledge you, the reader, for taking the time to read this story. Hopefully our joint efforts and passion for selling will continue to elevate the profession and inspire others to reach new heights in their careers.

1

Debunking Sales Myths

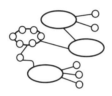

My name is Adam. I am a salesman.

I used to admit this reluctantly because nobody really wants to talk to a salesperson. If you are a fireman or a nurse, people flash admiring looks and ask questions about your work. But if you tell people you're a salesperson, they run away, figuring your only goal is to take their money.

I didn't plan on becoming a salesman, in the same way tax collectors probably didn't plan on becoming tax collectors and bus drivers thought they would grow up to be astronauts. There is nothing wrong with these professions, except that they weren't the dream jobs of childhood. The truth is that I prepared poorly in college for a career and simply settled on a job as a salesperson because I wasn't qualified to do anything else. Thus my career started as an accident.

After I took that first job in Sales, I was convinced it symbolized early life failure. And I know that wasn't my imagination getting the better of me. Even salespeople don't want to be called salespeople. They know of the widely-held stereotypes that salespeople are selfish, manipulative, and as ethical as ambulance-chasing lawyers. In response, sales managers and salespeople reject the term "salesperson" in favor of job titles designed to upgrade the status of the profession—"investment advisor," "specialist," or "territory manager," to name a few.

All right, Adam, you're probably thinking. *Why are you telling me this?* Because something happened to me—something extraordinary. If you had told me when I first became a salesperson that my new job was the first step on the path to enlightenment, I would have laughed. But that's exactly what happened, and I'm going to tell you how. I went from being an angry young man stuck in a job he hated to a man with a career he loves. I've defeated the ceaseless pressure of the sales profession and learned to embrace my work. I didn't complete this journey on my own—I had help from a very special man. But I'm getting ahead of myself. This story begins much earlier than that, and it is there that I will start.

The first company I worked for was called Spartan Windows, where they gave me the title of "account executive." This description, of course, relieved me of being called a salesperson. But I still dreaded waking up and going to work every morning.

At Spartan, I worked for Joe Moretti, a manager who embodied the quintessential stereotype of salespeople. He treated the sales process as a rigorous athletic competition, applying pressure to clients and employees without the slightest finesse. He saw each human interaction as a win−lose challenge and had a keen knack for making people uncomfortable, including me.

Joe was stuck in the seventies, both mentally and physically. He looked more like a mafia loan shark than a sales manager. His jet-black hair was slicked back with ample amounts of pomade. He wore double-breasted pinstripe suits adorned with hideous ties that featured orange and green jungle scenes. He added to his image by negotiating for a shiny black Cadillac as his company vehicle, even though all the other salespeople drove far less ostentatious cars. I didn't know whether to hate him or feel sorry for him. Okay, that's not true. I hated him.

You are probably wondering, *how did Joe come to be hired as a sales manager in the first place?* Joe had inherited a territory that was thriving and serviced the account base for years. When a new sales manager was needed, enough time had passed that nobody considered that Joe had never opened up the accounts that had produced all the results. I think Joe received the job because of his bravado and good looks. During his interview, there is no doubt he assured the company executives that he could whip the sales team into shape. They bought into his hype and assumed that salespeople would eagerly respond to the pressure from one of their former peers.

Joe liked to say that people will "walk through fire for a great leader." He probably used that line in the interview with the boast that he was that type of leader. Instead, few of the salespeople would have crossed the street with a glass of water if the jerk were on fire. I know that that sounds harsh and angry, but the truth was that many of us didn't care for him. That being said, I have since come to be grateful that I had Joe as my first manager. If it weren't for him, I wouldn't have embarked on a journey that led to so much positive change.

That journey began the day that he verbally ambushed me at our annual sales meeting.

"Adam?" Joe barked from the front of the room, with his twisted mix of false cheer and intimidation. "What do you think? Is it doable? Are you in?"

Darn it! I was caught in bobble-head mode and hadn't heard a word he had said. Bobble-head mode is when you nod your head up and down, pretending to listen, while your mind wanders. You've probably experienced it with clients in the middle of a business meeting and then you panic, hoping that the client doesn't ask your opinion of the last thing he just said. My wife catches me in it sometimes when she's talking about fabrics or decorating and calls it "selective hearing." But it's definitely not supposed to happen in the middle of the annual sales meeting. I was stumped. I had no idea what Joe had asked of me. The eyes of seventeen other salespeople and corporate executives were cast my way. I froze, hoping that my surprise did not register. Seconds felt like weeks. I finally concluded that it was in my best interest to show the unbridled enthusiasm expected at a sales pep rally.

"I AM in!" I said, mustering the necessary bravado while wondering what exactly I had volunteered for. I quickly descended from embarrassment to shock when I realized that Joe was establishing our sales goals for the coming year.

"Excellent!" Joe shouted, writing my goal on the flip chart. "We're putting Adam down for a thirty-percent sales increase. I sure hope you're up to the challenge after the terrible results you brought in last year!" Joe laughed, and I looked around the table as my colleagues smiled awkwardly, sympathy for me warring with their desire to please Joe.

Joe regularly set goals for the coming year in this ridiculous and arbitrary fashion. *We might as well throw darts at a board*, I thought. Unlike bosses who motivated their employees by being good role models and leading by example, Joe believed that establishing unrealistic goals maximized results by keeping us constantly on edge. Instead, we inadvertently transferred the pressure to customers, producing the opposite of Joe's objectives.

Joe's overconfidence was vexing because he demonstrated none of the selling skills he insisted were lacking in others. If I asked how to achieve his lofty expectations, his answer remained, "I expect you to figure it out. You're the salesperson and we pay you for results. If you can't get the results, then I have the wrong guy."

I sank down in my chair, wondering if Joe could achieve the goals he had foisted on me. Was he just setting me up for another year of failure? *It's easy for you to criticize my results when you're not the one responsible for achieving them*, I thought, as Joe shouted and carried on at the front of the room. The truth is, Joe was like a backseat driver—looking at past results without providing a roadmap to help the driver reach the destination.

There has to be a better way to lead people, I thought. *But how? And why do I care? I don't even like my job. Are all sales managers as inept as Joe? Where does he find those awful ties with orange lions and purple monkeys? Crap! I'm in bobble head mode again! I better start listening in case he calls on me.*

The next phase of the sales meeting was Joe's training class. Here, Joe stressed a linear, step-by-step process that works best when customers cooperate and allow salespeople to control the meeting. Too bad that almost never happens. Joe was also obsessed with open-ended questions and thought they were the key to sales.

Almost every sales training program stresses the power of open-ended questions. But, in my experience, open-ended questions didn't always work. I wondered if this was yet another of Joe's outdated approaches—just another theory that enabled sales trainers to profess superior knowledge over their students.

An open-ended question begins with the words *who, what, when, how,* or *why,* thus (theoretically) requiring an answer longer than a simple "yes" or "no." Closed-ended questions were the kind that got you that one-word answer—or at least that is what we were always being taught.

The prevailing myth in sales was that open-ended questions were the only way to get the client talking. Thanks to my experience in the field, however, I was beginning to realize that the key issue wasn't the kind of questions you were asking; it was *listening* to the client's answers. In the right situations, closed-ended questions could be just as effective as those highly praised open-ended ones. As long as the client understood you were listening carefully, the questions themselves could be phrased in any way that best suited the situation.

So, it wasn't so much the kind of question that was important as it was the information that you could get from the client that really mattered.

As the rest of the sales meeting progressed, I sat silently without paying attention to another word Joe said. My fate was sealed. I hadn't just been assigned another year of unrealistic sales expectations. I'd volunteered for it. There was no end in sight.

Adam, you're a bobble-head idiot, I thought. But it wasn't entirely my fault, was it?

As my focus on the meeting dwindled, I began to remember my first days at Spartan Windows, when Joe had "trained" me to do sales.

Joe only coached me for three days during my tenure at Spartan. *Coaching* would be a generous term, though. Instead of coaching or teaching me, he took over sales calls and irritated my customers with his pushiness. He was more interested in feeding his ego than nurturing my professional development. After a client meeting, he'd nudge me with his elbow and tell me how he'd "worked" the client. During every sales call, he'd ask, "Can we have an order today?"

It's not a terrible question. But when it's asked by an overzealous, inept salesperson? Trust me. It doesn't work.

Joe gave me what he insisted were "insider" tips. In fairness to him, though, he wasn't the only one to blame for this faulty approach. Joe was simply repeating the vapid platitudes that have been shared by sales managers and salespeople for generations. They are the myths that sales professionals repeat mindlessly to mask incompetence. Managers are fond of saying things like...

"You have to ask for the order."

"Get them saying 'yes'!"

"The first 'no' is the beginning of the sale."

"You have to become your customer's best friend."

"The only good question is an 'open-ended' question."

...and a bunch of other drivel like that. I eventually learned that these are just sales myths, which fail to portray reality.

During one of our days in the field, Joe winked at me before we went into a sales call. "Watch and learn," he said with a smirk. In the meeting, he riddled my potential new client with a litany of pre-scripted, open-ended questions.

The meeting quickly deteriorated into a manipulative chess game. Joe was determined to prove there was no way the prospect could survive another day without Spartan Windows.

"How are things going with your current window supplier?" he asked.

"Fine."

Joe waited for elaboration to his open-ended question. It never came. "I mean," Joe persisted, "if there was one thing you could change to make them a better supplier to you, what would you change?"

Silence...

"Honestly," the prospect said, after some consideration, "they do a nice job. I like the product. Our salespeople, who resell the product to builders and remodelers, like it. The service is great and I really like the salesperson who calls on us. He's probably the best rep we've ever had!"

The customer's meaning should have been clear to any salesperson—but Joe was not any salesperson. He lived by 1980s slogans of sales persistence. Instead of taking the hint, he bombarded the prospect with more open-ended questions. "What do they do to help you grow? What would you say they should improve about their design features? In what ways could they improve deliveries?"

Good questions; bad timing.

Joe persisted until the irritated prospect told us to leave his office. Follow-up sales calls would be futile. Joe's manipulative open-ended questions had burned that bridge. More importantly, the sales call proved to me that the open-ended question theory and—by association, most of the theories expressed in sales myths—were incomplete. Open-ended questions are a subset of the skills necessary to fully understand a client's needs, not the sum total of the process.

Even Joe knew the meeting went poorly but still had the audacity to blame the prospect for the outcome. "He wasn't being truthful with us," Joe rationalized. "I know he has some problems, even if he didn't admit it. I'm sure we made some headway. You should follow up with him in a few weeks."

Did we just sit in the same meeting? I wondered. I saw an angry prospect, while Joe believed his questions were perfect. I observed sales aggression, while Joe thought he had demonstrated professionalism. He assured me that his methods would work on sales calls later that day. *Oh joy,* I thought as we drove I-94 through the Chicago Loop. *I can't wait to be a part of those meetings.*

I was sure Joe's blind faith in sales myths didn't really work. I am not against open-ended questions. They are hugely valuable in the process of qualifying a prospect, but nonetheless they are not the sum total of it. I knew there had to be a better way to do my job—I just didn't know what it was. That awful sales meeting was a catalyst.

I finally realized nothing would change as long as I reported to a man with bad selling skills. Joe was trying to pass himself off as a guru who knew all the answers. He drove around in his fancy car with no idea of how ridiculous he looked. He thought all the answers were in material rewards, not satisfaction with a job well done. And he was no guru. He wasn't even a mediocre teacher. I was pretty sure even then that I knew the difference, and I knew I wanted something more. Sure, a nice car and a nice house can be great, but I wanted to feel satisfaction in my work. I wanted to do something meaningful.

I'd had great teachers in my life, like the professional golf instructor who taught me how to enjoy the game by focusing on the right habits. He was calm, competent, insightful, inspiring—everything that Joe wasn't. He never criticized where my golf shot landed. He never said, "That stunk. Come on! Hit it 300 yards. You can do it!" He never asked me to produce results beyond my capabilities. Instead, he focused on helping me understand the proper form of a golf swing.

My golf instructor would frequently make a correction to my swing even though some shots were exactly on target. Sometimes my results were so abysmal I was ready to give up the game. Rather than criticize, my teacher noted the aspects of my swing worth repeating.

He emphasized the importance of developing dependable techniques. "You've had some nice results out of pure luck. I'd rather you have some modest accomplishments on purpose than succeed by accident. I can teach you to repeat on purpose. An accident is always an accident." I noticed that he rarely watched where my ball landed. Instead, he observed the trajectory. I realized that, by studying the position of my hands and body, he knew the outcome of each shot before it even happened.

In spite of my golf teacher's valuable instruction, I experienced feelings of frustration similar to those I had when failing to achieve sales quotas. During one especially difficult lesson, I admitted to my golf instructor that I was getting increasingly angry with my scores. He laughed. "I'll tell you what. Why don't you stop worrying about that? Let me think about your score. You focus on your swing. You've had some shots that are spectacular. You'll build on that."

His words calmed me. By the end of that lesson, I was striking the ball better than ever. I was invigorated with the same emotion I experienced as an adolescent when my dad helped me with a perplexing algebra problem. Abject frustration and self-doubt gave way to happiness and joy as I overcame a difficult challenge.

A professional golfer does not improve her performance by studying only the trajectory of the golf ball. Instead, she creates consistent results by studying her golf *swing* and how it corresponds to the trajectory of the golf ball. This lesson seemed just as applicable to sales. Joe was focused on results but unable to identify the performance habits that would create them. Criticizing my results didn't do anything to improve my game. What mattered was improving the process. Working on my swing changed my game and produced tremendous results. It stood to reason that working on my sales behavior would change my sales results. *Success isn't an accident*, I thought. *It's something you do.*

Two possible responses occur in the face of challenge. One is the fear-based, fight-or-flight response triggered by the base of your brain in the medulla oblongata. The other is a positive emotional response triggered by activation of the brain's frontal cortex. In the former, challenges are viewed as threats, causing your body to produce adrenalin, cortisol, and other chemicals that inhibit learning. Conversely, the decision to treat challenges as learning opportunities triggers the frontal cortex to produce dopamine, serotonin, and other neurotransmitters that create happiness and even feelings of euphoria.

I didn't realize at the time that I could *choose* which portion of my brain to exercise. The golf instructor, my late father, and other good teachers helped me unknowingly use my frontal cortex. A bad instructor, like Joe, inhibits learning by instilling fear.

I wanted to be excellent at my job, but I would never achieve excellence at Spartan Windows. I needed a real sales instructor.

During one of the last sales calls I made at Spartan, I asked a closed-ended question to a potential new dealer: "Are things going okay with your current supplier?" I knew it was a closed-ended question and could be answered with a "yes" or "no." But I also knew that an open-ended question could be answered with a terse "fine" or "not so good." The important thing was that I show genuine interest in the dealer, not force an open-ended question and end up sounding manipulative or like a psychotherapist. I concluded that people would talk regardless of the question, as long as you keep the conversation *conversational*.

Prior to the question, the prospect and I had just finished lunch, during which he discussed his business plan and long-term goals. I listened. We talked about his ownership challenges, the market outlook, and how he was trying to motivate his salespeople. I listened more. Our rapport was strong, so I eventually figured it was a good time to ask about his current supplier. I thought back to the lessons I'd learned from the golf pro. What mattered here was the process—in this case, the process of listening, not questioning.

My instincts were perfect, because the information I obtained with that closed-ended question was beyond my wildest dreams. He said, "The reason I wanted to have lunch is so I can know you—to conduct a sort of interview with you as my potential new salesperson. I need someone who understands my challenges. Things are going horribly wrong with our current supplier— delivery screw-ups, product problems, and, truthfully, I don't like my salesperson very much."

Now, I ask you! Which sales call would you rather be on: one where you ask perfectly phrased open-ended questions and get nowhere, or one where you simply listen to a man spill his heart and finish up with an angry condemnation of your competitor?

As you might expect, that lunch conversation evolved into a sale. The company was Benton Distribution.

During that final, terrible annual sales meeting where Joe had ambushed me, I wondered, as Joe prattled in the front of the room, whether Jack Benton would stay loyal to me if I switched employers.

It doesn't matter, I thought. *I'm quitting anyway. I have to find a better way to do this.*

Joe taught from the boilerplate trainer's guide and my colleagues dutifully filled in their workbooks like good soldiers. No one around me was willing to question what Joe was telling us—after all, Joe was just repeating the same information that has been given to salespeople for generations. Joe was teaching us things to do, but I knew he wasn't teaching us the right things to do.

I needed to know why certain actions produced the desired results. I wanted to learn more than the traditional myths of the profession. I believed I could have a career that meant something to me, something bigger than expensive cars or overpriced dinners at fancy restaurants. But I needed a real teacher.

An accident is always an accident, I thought. *I want success on purpose.* That was my new mantra.

2

The Insatiable Desire for More

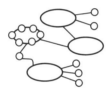

That night, when I got home from the sales meeting, my wife, Mary, was sitting quietly at the kitchen table grading papers. Her calm demeanor belied the disappointment she had in her students' work. She scribbled comments in red pen, wielding it as a sword that her students should fear if they slacked on the job. We kissed "hello" and I began creating my orange chicken stir-fry with broccoli. As I slid the chicken into hot oil, I told Mary about my big decision.

"I'm quitting on Monday," I said over the crackle of the sizzling wok. "The only reason I didn't quit on the spot," I assured her, "was that I didn't want to make a fool of myself."

"Well, that's good," Mary said with a hint of cynicism. Mary and I had been married for six years. Her thick, shoulder-length red hair contrasts with blue eyes that twinkle like sapphires when she smiles. I fell in love with those eyes, her smarts, and her determination the first moment we met at a campus party during our junior year at Michigan. What she saw in me? Well, you'll have to ask her.

Mary's a tough cookie and has never been one to complain. She's never sympathized with whiners and told me once, "I never accept an invitation to someone's 'pity party.'" She can be sweet and kind when she wants, but when she's angry, her Irish passion is revealed with a stare that can shake you like a bolt of lightning.

Mary stands just over five feet tall, but she projects power through her perfect posture. She doesn't yell but instead talks with a soft intensity that captivates. I've rarely seen her buckle under pressure, and she's never been timid about putting me in my place. Even at the peak of anger, she remains rational in her arguments, an ability of hers that I envy and to which I have fallen victim many times. "Why are you so angry?" she asked me.

"Joe's a jerk."

"Then find a new job."

"I plan to," I said defensively. She raised an eyebrow at me.

"The people at Spartan think highly of you. If you quit, what happens then?"

"I find a new job," I told her.

"What will a new employer think of hiring someone without a job? What would it do to your reputation in the industry? Are you going to be happy without a paycheck for who-knows-how-long?"

She was right, of course—but I wasn't thinking rationally. I was thinking about the long-term future I wanted while ignoring the reality of the present. I didn't want only job security; I wanted a career that I could feel passionate about. How could I make Mary understand that, to me, the risk was worth it? Mary was my most important ally. I had to get her on my side.

"What was so terrible?" she asked, softening a little. She knew there was more to the story than a bad day at work.

"I was humiliated by Joe, along with every other salesperson in the company."

"He can't humiliate you without your permission."

"I know. You're right. It's just—Mary, I'm not happy. I want to be doing something bigger. I need a new job."

She sighed and came over to me at the stove. "Okay, then," she said with finality. "Let's put your resume together and get you the next great job in your life. Deal?"

I smiled. She kissed me on the cheek and stood with her arm around my waist while I stirred in the broccoli. "Deal," I said.

I was cleansed by a flood of optimism. I was heading to a better place, with the greatest woman in the world at my back. I recognized this emotion. I'd experienced it solving those problems with my dad and perfecting my swing with the golf instructor: it was joy, the sense of gratification that emanates from accomplishment.

Martin Seligman, the former president of the American Psychological Association, illustrated the difference between pleasure and gratification. You feel pleasure when you get a good result on your test, taste a piece of moist chocolate cake, or make a lucky golf shot. Gratification is the satisfaction you achieve from *studying* for the test, *baking* a cake, or *knowing* the mechanics of the golf swing. Pleasure is the result; gratification is the process. Pleasure is temporary; gratification is lasting. Gratification produces joy.

I wondered if there were ways to feel joy in the selling profession. It's not exactly an occupation that promotes spiritual happiness. The profession violates every law of spirituality by creating a constant and insatiable desire for more. Last year's success is nullified, becoming the challenge of a thirty-percent increase next year. Even the salesperson of the year, after receiving an evening of accolades, must venture into the harsh world of business to get "more."

Selling is a career without credentials. It's not like being a doctor or a lawyer, professions that require certifications and licenses. Instead, salespeople are measured by the results they achieve, which, truth be told, can be purely accidental. If you think that achieving results proves a salesperson is competent, you would be wrong.

I was living proof of the phenomenon. I was like a paper towel salesman calling on the local grocery store chain. I sold a product to people who resold it to their customers. I could be bad at my job due to the fortunate circumstance of having successful resellers. I am in no way denying the importance of achieving results but merely stating that you *can* get good results even with bad skills.

I enjoyed a nice salary, decent commissions, a company car, and a 401k program with company matching. Even though I failed to achieve Joe's unrealistic goals, my sales were increasing and I was considered a rising star at Spartan. I could have ridden that path for many years and built a comfortable life. If materialism was the benchmark, I was leading a successful life. But everything I learned in church taught me that the pursuit of material wealth was not a path to happiness.

I discovered it wasn't only my church lessons. I remembered a quote I'd read by Rabbi Hyman Schachtel, who said, "Happiness is wanting what you have, not having what you want." I wondered why my career couldn't be more like the wisdom of Rabbi Schachtel. I didn't want to be like Joe, throwing money around to hide the emptiness inside me. I didn't want to be like my coworkers, following Joe's asinine directives without questioning anything or thinking for themselves. I wanted to be good at my job—not by accident, but on purpose. I wanted to feel joy in the work I was doing. I wanted to be a leader, not a follower.

I decided to seek the answer. I was on a quest to find gratification in the sales profession. Fortunately,

I was about to meet a mentor who would start me on that path—a man who would change the course of my life forever.

3

In Search of Growth

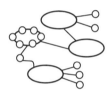

The morning after my conversation with Mary, I got to work—I had an hour before I needed to leave for Spartan. While eating my corn flakes, I picked up that day's issue (October 15, 1996) of the *Chicago Tribune* and scanned every classified ad that I could find for sales jobs. My anxiety grew as I perused one classified ad after another, realizing that most of the positions were way out of my league. It seemed my ambition outstripped my experience.

"Don't forget to check CareerBuilder.com," Mary said as she pulled a pink V-neck sweater over her white blouse. She gathered up her coat and canvas Field Museum tote bag before whisking herself out the door.

"Yes, dear."

After Mary closed the door, I hefted my new $4,195 IBM ThinkPad onto the dining room table and fired it up. I finished my morning coffee and scanned a few more pages of the Tribune while the static of the dial-up modem completed its connection to the Internet. Then I used my Netscape browser to land at the CareerBuilder site, wondering what I would find with this newfangled classified ad service. *More sales jobs out of my league?* I asked myself.

Finally, among a handful of sales jobs, I found one listing that seemed promising. A window company was seeking a sales representative with five years of experience and a college degree. I was a little short on experience, but it was the only job for which I was closely qualified. I wrote a quick cover letter and emailed the resume Mary had polished the night before.

Seven days later, a call came from Abe Isaacson. You may recall the ill-fated sales meeting I'd attended with Joe—the one where the client had ultimately thrown us out of his office. That prospect said his salesperson was the "best he ever had." The salesperson he referred to was Abe, the Acme regional sales manager.

Abe kept his home office scrupulously tidy. His desk was bare except for a computer, a leather-bound appointment book, and a framed photo of a stately woman in her fifties who must have been his wife. Abe himself was well-dressed but not flashy, with bright, blue-grey eyes and a head of curly, silver-grey hair above his high, intelligent forehead. His shoulders slumped slightly forward—I later learned this was because he was an avid cyclist. He wasn't particularly handsome, but he had an approachable, almost informal air that immediately put me at ease. His quiet confidence was contagious.

Abe described the job in detail, explaining that his new salesperson would be calling on a network of existing dealers who resold the Acme product. He said it would be necessary to bring value to those dealers by producing new sales leads for them. I particularly loved a comment he made about becoming a sales consultant to clients. He said, "Any salesman can push windows onto his customer's dock. A great salesman helps his clients move the product out their front doors." This was the job I wanted.

Next, Abe got right down to business. "Well, Adam," he said. "I'd like you to tell me about your sales philosophy." I was thrown. I'd never thought of sales as something that *had* a philosophy.

I lamely said with feigned confidence, "I think being honest and helpful is the key to selling. Return phone calls. Be on time. I think those are the key things to selling. And I think my clients really like me because I do whatever it takes to keep them happy." Abe asked me more questions about how I approached my day-to-day responsibilities, and I realized, to my embarrassment, that I had degenerated into boasting rather than describing my actual behaviors. Every time I opened my mouth, it got worse. I was blowing the interview.

As the interview drifted toward my last chance to make an impression, Abe asked, "How do you close?"

Hooray! I knew this one. I only had to recite one of the sales myths. I started to repeat one of the mantras I'd learned at Spartan, but then I paused. I'd figured that I had little to lose at that point; why not just be honest? "I know I'm supposed to say that I 'ask for the order.' But truthfully, I don't know if I've ever asked for the order directly." I stopped.

Abe waited.

I scoured my brain to recall how I closed deals. I couldn't think of a specific technique. "I guess I have a lot to learn about sales. I've had some decent sales. They took time and persistence... and um... I don't have a specific answer... I just try to make each meeting count and... I guess that's my answer." My cheeks were burning. There went any chance I'd had of impressing this guy. *There will be more interviews,* I told myself. *This is just practice.*

Abe nodded politely and wrote a note. I sat uncomfortably in the spacious office, waiting to be dismissed. I figured Abe would promise to be in touch, tell me I was a good candidate, and later send me the rejection letter.

Instead of throwing me out of his office, he studied my face. "It's better to know and think you don't than to not know and think you do," he said.

I stared at him. "I like that a lot. How did you come up with it?"

He assured me he wasn't smart enough to make that one up. "The Tao philosopher, Lao Tzu, said it over twenty-five hundred years ago."

Abe set his notepad aside to put me at ease and spoke kindly. "I'm interested in understanding your innate talents, Adam. My goal is to know what type of raw material you're made of. Let me ask again: Do you have *any* philosophy about selling?" I barely understood his question; clearly he knew that my previous answer was smoke and mirrors, a desperate attempt to prove I had the right stuff. I began wondering, along with Abe, if I had the raw material.

That's all a beginner, in any endeavor, really is—raw material. Every expert has failed as a beginner, at one point, before achieving greatness. In order to achieve greatness, the expert must first endure the hardships of trial and error to learn which actions produce the right results. In spite of my own doubts, I hoped to convince Abe that I had the right raw material.

"Well... I was taught a step-by-step process. It's supposed to lead people toward a buying decision. But, I feel it's unrealistic."

"Interesting."

"What's interesting?" I asked.

"That you think it's *unrealistic*. What do you mean by that?"

"It's logical on paper, but I don't think it's how things happen. Can I draw it for you?"

"Please do!"

I laid out the seven steps of the linear process I had been taught.

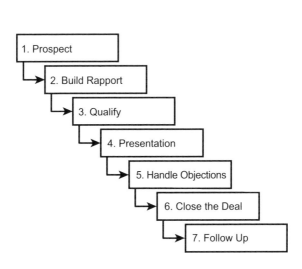

1. Prospect
2. Build Rapport
3. Qualify
4. Presentation
5. Handle Objections
6. Close the Deal
7. Follow Up

I described the actions I had learned for each step. For example, I was taught to build rapport by discussing something in the client's office, such as a picture or trophy. I told him that the qualifying process stressed open-ended questions, which I believed were overrated. I also described the feature-benefit presentation format we had been taught at Spartan. I added a few other points, before concluding that only some of the ideas made sense to me. He perused the diagram before turning the paper over.

"Here's how I see it," he began. "This process you laid out has been the prevailing theory for over a century. It was a good start, but it's dated. I agree with you that the logic doesn't portray reality.

"Selling is part linear, but not all linear. Everybody wants the selling process to offer guaranteed outcomes.

But each situation is unique; one sale is easy while another takes more time and effort. It's unrealistic to expect that you can win every sale. You can't control the minds and actions of other people. So you need a model that's real and that produces the greatest chance of success."

Abe drew his own diagram.

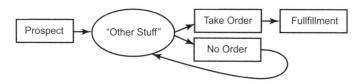

"Every sale begins with a prospect. That's obvious. You may bump into someone by chance at a neighborhood social or, more likely, invest a hundred or more hours making phone calls to meet the right candidate. Either way, you meet someone new. That much is linear. No sales process can begin until you have a prospect. So there *is* a step one, which is to find a prospect."

I was too distracted by the daunting vision of *one hundred hours making phone calls* to fully process what he was saying. Was he serious?

"Then you have dialogue," he continued. "Sometimes the dialogue lasts a minute and sometimes it lasts years. The dialogue is a conversation in words, actions, voice mails, and so forth. It usually includes a product demonstration, some persuasion. Eventually discussions lead to something... or nothing. If your conversation leads to something, you take the order and, as I like to say, you fulfill a promise.

"A lot of sales training teaches 'follow-up,' just like you worded it in the last step of your linear diagram. But follow-up often involves fixing a problem that could have been avoided. Fulfillment is different. I use the term *fulfillment* because it implies a lot about what you did earlier in the process."

"What is the difference between fulfillment and follow-up?" I asked.

"Let's say you have a client who expected a delivery, and it's late. He's angry. Has that happened to you?"

"Yeah. Too many times!"

"You probably told your client a standard lead time, which he cut close by ordering at the last minute. More accurately described, he procrastinated and ordered too late, and it's *your* fault," Abe said. "You end up jumping through hoops, involving an entire organization in the fire drill, wondering why you didn't just get the order a week or two earlier. It's frustrating. Agreed?"

"Yep," I admitted with a smile. "That's happened a few times, but not just to me. Most salespeople in my company spend time putting out fires."

"It's a common mistake. You tell the client it will take 'three to four weeks.' The client hears *three*. You really want *five* and he gives you *two!*"

I laughed. His point was right on target.

"You had no chance to get the product on time," he said. "Fulfillment was destroyed in the presentation phase. You should have told your client the specific date you needed to get the order. So 'putting out fires' is good follow-up, but it's usually wasted energy. The client *will* get the order late. There *will* be apologies and unnecessary costs, and time *will* be wasted. That's follow-up.

"Fulfillment," he explained, "happens proactively when you realize there are ways to avoid many problems before they occur. In this case, fulfillment would have been to tell the client he needed to give you five weeks in order to avoid problems later on."

I nodded.

"Follow-up can be fulfillment *or* putting out fires, depending on how you handled the early stages of the sales process. Fulfillment is a satisfied client who never dealt with a fire in the first place. Make sense?"

"Yes. It seems simple."

"It *is* simple, but challenging. You have to be willing to advise your clients and make sure they take your good advice," Abe said.

He pointed to his diagram. "Sometimes the initial sales process goes slowly and you get no order. Then, you decide whether or not you want to keep the dialogue running. If so, it's back to the drawing board for more discussions, questions, presentations, and so forth. That's why I call it 'other stuff.' It's non-linear. It's simple to understand, and yet it takes a lifetime to master." He gave me a knowing, mischievous grin. I was really starting to like this guy. *Man,* I thought, *I want this job.*

"So what you're saying is..." I paused, wanting to get this right. "I need to be more focused on the relationship with the client, and perfecting all the details that will make that relationship run smoothly?"

"Perfect!" he said, beaming with delight as he leaned back in his chair. "Non-linear selling. Take care of the customers. Help them make wise decisions. The transactions will come organically. That's it. All the activity between the time you meet a prospect and take the order is the 'other stuff.'"

"Non-linear selling," I repeated. "Wow. I like that."

He smiled. "I thought you would. Here, let me draw you another diagram."

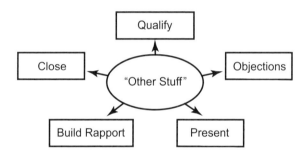

"The other stuff includes all the things you've learned," he explained. "The steps materialize when prospects are ready, in the order *they* choose. If someone wants to hand you an order, only a fool would say, 'Hold on! I haven't finished my presentation.'"

I chuckled. "I think I've seen some salespeople do exactly that."

"Sometimes you're able to use each step in a linear progression. Usually, you aren't. If you start thinking of sales as a non-linear process, you'll be more prepared to deal with situations as they arise.

"Now," he continued, "you acquire new business in three different ways. First, you seek new customers. Second, you call on existing customers to sell them products they already buy. Third, you introduce new products to existing customers. It's very complex, actually, but the Non-Linear Sales Formula simplifies the process. It describes reality. It illustrates how you re-use the same skills repeatedly with new and existing clients. Does that make sense to you?"

"It does," I said. I wasn't just parroting answers, trying to impress him. It *did* make sense.

"It works in all aspects of selling," Abe said, "but I use the business-to-business example because it's easiest to understand."

"How *would* this apply to consumer selling? I don't see a fit."

He grinned and rubbed his hands together, preparing to answer my challenge. I laughed out loud at his enthusiasm. "Let's say you sell cars for a living," he said. "Most car salespeople see the sale as a transactional event rather than a relationship. If the salesperson closes the deal, the transaction is done and the relationship ends; fulfillment is someone else's responsibility. If the salesperson does not close on the first call, the transaction is *still* done; he moves on to the next prospect. Either way, the interaction is a one-time event."

"A top performer sees it differently. She accepts that she might not close the deal on the first meeting. She follows up with prospects after they leave the dealership. When she makes the sale, it is not the end of the transaction; it's the beginning of a new relationship. It's the *first* car she will sell a long-term client. She sees referral opportunities and a relationship to build on.

"In retail selling, there is a buying cycle that top performers acknowledge. They strive to be in communication when an existing client is ready for the repeat purchase of a product. For example, many clients lease a new car every three or four years. It amazes me that salespeople neglect to follow up when a client leases a car. The salesperson knows the *exact day* a client will lease the next car, yet neglects to be in touch with the client to capture that sale. Top sales performers keep the dialogue running with clients and prospects, in this case keeping in contact with the client to start discussing plans when his or her lease runs out. Top sales leaders apply the Non-Linear Sales Formula in all situations.

"Selling skills are part of a tool kit that you build. You pull out the right tool for the right application. You do the best thing you can in each situation." Abe paused. "Of course, many salespeople never learn. The commitment to learning is a decision. You can achieve twenty years of learning—or you can repeat one year of experience twenty times."

"I think I work with guys who keep repeating the first year," I said.

Abe smiled. Maybe I wasn't totally blowing this interview after all.

"What other questions do you have?" he asked.

"What makes your products special?"

He winked. "I don't think there is anything special about them at all. A window is a window."

The disappointment registered on my face, so he elaborated.

"We make an excellent product. A lot of companies do. I respect my competition. The truth is that I respect your current employer, Spartan Windows, and believe *they* make a great product. Don't you?"

"Yes," I said. I *did* think our product was as good as Acme's.

"But you have to ask yourself the more important question: 'Why does Acme outsell you four to one in the market?'"

He had a point. "Good question! Why do you?"

Abe smiled without divulging anything. "Good question, grasshopper."

Clearly, he wasn't going to spill his secrets unless he hired me. I was beginning to realize how much I could learn from this compelling, enigmatic man. "I'd really like to work for you," I blurted.

"Then I have one more question for you," Abe said. "What is it that you want? Why would you quit one window company just to work for another? What are you seeking?"

"I want to learn. I want growth."

"You want to be promoted?" Abe asked.

"Sure," I said. "I guess every salesperson wants to be promoted one day. But I meant that I want to *grow*. I guess there are two kinds of growth, now that I think about it.

One is the kind where you get a new title on your business card. The other is the type of growth where you develop the skills that create security in your career. I want the second type of growth."

Abe smiled and said, "Good answer. I can help you find that."

4

Career Security

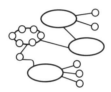

"How did it go?" Mary asked that night over my specialty, chicken paprikash, a dish handed down from my Hungarian grandmother. I told her I botched the interview. "Hmm," she said. As usual, I had no idea what she was thinking.

"I felt a real rapport with this guy," I said. "I really want to work for him."

Mary smiled. "If it's meant to be, it'll happen," she said. I wished I had her faith.

⌣

During the week I didn't hear from Abe, I concluded that my chances to work for him were dwindling. I went on two other interviews with the same blustery, unappealing version of Joe, men who wanted me to repeat the same tired mantras shouted during every Spartan sales meeting. Then, just when I felt sure that any other manager would be just like Joe and I'd be stuck working a job I hated, the phone rang. It was Abe offering me a second interview. "Of course," I said in response. "I'd be thrilled to come in again." I wondered if he could hear the excitement in my voice. Mary smirked when I told her.

"I told you so," she said.

"You did no such thing!" I protested. She rolled her eyes.

"It's your turn to do the laundry," she said.

I dressed to impress for my second interview with Abe. But maybe I shouldn't have bothered—I could have sworn he was wearing the same loose-fitting grey suit, white shirt and plain dark tie I first saw him in. He jumped right into the interview as if I last saw him a few minutes ago, not a week earlier.

"What if I told you that your answer to my interview question was perfectly accurate?"

"Which answer?" I asked.

"The answer to my question, 'How do you close?'"

I was dumbfounded. I had thought that was the question I'd answered the worst. "It was?"

"Oh, yes. I interviewed nine candidates. I enjoyed your answer the most. It was honest. You've learned the sales secret."

"I have? If so, then it's a secret to me." I intended no joke, but Abe laughed anyway.

I waited for him to explain what the secret was, but he switched gears. "The best predictor of future performance is always past behavior," he professed confidently. "A leopard doesn't change its spots. People always promise to build new habits *after* getting a great job opportunity. But I figure, why take a chance? I would rather just hire people who already have the right habits. Show me a person with the right habits and I can teach a method that works. Make sense?"

I nodded. During the next ninety minutes, he grilled me with a series of questions to reveal signs of self-discipline. He asked me about my organizational habits and periods in life when I'd dealt with challenging situations. He tossed out hypothetical questions and then followed up by asking about my real-life performance to verify whether my answers matched the actions I promised in those hypothetical situations. He was deftly discovering the truth of who I was—the raw material.

Abe asked surprisingly few questions about my sales habits. After nearly two hours, he finally stopped taking notes and closed his portfolio. I had been through an intense interrogation, although I never once felt defensive. Abe seemed to be rooting for me. He hadn't told me any of the answers he was looking for, but I felt sure some of his questions were intended to help me find them within myself. He wanted to know what made me tick. By the time we finished, he discovered, among other things, how I put myself through college, coached an unstable co-worker from anger to calm, captained my intramural softball team to two championships, and redesigned Spartan's sales database when the company refused to allocate the funding for the IT department to take care of it.

Abe asked real questions, probing questions that got to the root of who I was and what I believed in. Though he gave away nothing of himself in the interview, I had the strangest feeling that our conversation had brought us closer together.

At last, he leaned back in his chair. I was as exhausted as if I'd just run a marathon. "So, Adam. Do you think salespeople are born or made?"

I was caught off guard. It didn't seem like a trick question, but it was certainly not the casual chitchat his posture promised. I took a moment to ponder my answer. I remember Joe frequently saying that he was a "born" salesperson. So my first response was to negate Joe's audacious claim.

"Well, I've *heard* that they are born. But, in reality, I think they're made." Then I thought more about Joe. He was a career salesperson, but all the experience in the world never "made" him better at his job. "Maybe some people don't have the personality, though. So I guess you have to have the right personality, too." I finally concluded, "I'm not sure."

Abe regarded me pensively, a poker player not revealing his hand.

"What do you think?" I asked. "Are they born or made?"

"Yes," Abe said with sudden merriment while not immediately letting me in on his joke.

"Yes?"

"Yes, I think salespeople are born *and* made. Show me a great athlete and I will show you a person with a rare gift from God. At the same time, talent is not enough. The greatest athletes are intense students of their crafts. I think that great salespeople are no different. They combine natural talent with a desire for growth. Some people are born with more gifts than others. But those gifts are meaningless if the performer won't commit to learning the craft. Ability is the learned manifestation of talent."

He stopped. I waited.

Abe liked moments of silence. I had little to say, so I waited for him to speak.

"I notice that you wait in silence a lot when we talk, Adam," he said.

"I know," I confessed. "It's not that I have nothing of value to say. It's more that I am digesting interesting things for the first time. I figure that unless I have something really important to say, I ought to just be quiet for a moment."

"Try not to lose that trait as you learn to sell. It's a very good one!"

I had already realized that Abe was a salesperson with a special set of skills. His idea of non-linear sales went against everything I'd been taught. He also talked about avoiding conflict and reducing sales aggression. His concepts resonated with every experience I'd had in the field, although I previously had no words to describe my subconscious discoveries. Abe was giving them a voice that differed greatly from the faulty lessons I received at Spartan. Even Abe's presence differed enormously from the flashy suits and false bravado I often saw at Spartan.

In our interviews, Abe was gregarious but never boisterous. He was persuasive but never pushy. Nothing I said seemed to make him defensive or upset, even when I'd disagreed with him. I felt totally at ease around him.

"Do you have any last questions for me?" he asked, with his bluish grey eyes wide open, as if they were totally focused on the present.

"Well... you said my answer about closing the sale was the best one. I told my wife, Mary, that I lost my chance for the job with that question, so I'm a little surprised. What was good about it? What's the secret?"

"Adam, you already know it. The secret is that you don't need to learn to close sales. The secret is that you do the best thing for the client at a specific moment in time. Correct?"

"Yeah. I guess that's true."

"That's it," Abe said with finality. "That's all the detail I can provide for now. It's a subject to be explored at another time."

I thought his words implied I would get the job. Otherwise, why would he say, "We'll explore the subject later"? It made me feel a little bold and I expressed how badly I wanted to work for him. I also wanted him to know that I picked up the inference in his words. "Does that mean you're offering me a job?"

He laughed. "You have very good listening skills, Adam. That's the trait of a good salesperson...listening for the closing signals. But, no. I'm not offering you the job. I have a few other people to interview. I will tell you that you're a strong candidate. You will definitely go places in your life, Adam."

"So this means you're not going to share the secret with me?" I asked, smiling.

"If I tell you all my best sales ideas now and you keep working for my competitor, that wouldn't be very smart of me," he said.

He had a point.

It seemed very possible that he was going to hire me, but that last statement made me uncomfortable. Abe was not the type of person I wanted to compete against. I wanted to be on his team.

That night, I told Mary how difficult the interview was. "I *think* he liked me. At least until the end."

She laughed, "He liked you and then he stopped liking you?"

"No! I mean I think he liked me the whole time. Up until the end of the interview, I believed he was going to hire me. But when I asked if I was getting the job, he hesitated and I wasn't sure anymore."

"You worry too much," she said. "I'm sure you did fine. If this doesn't work out, another job will come along."

"I know. But this guy is really different." I tried to think of how I could explain what I'd felt in the interview to Mary. Abe's presence was so compelling. It wasn't something I could put into words, but I'd understood that I was interacting with someone special. "I think I could learn a lot from him," I said finally. "More than I've ever learned from anyone else."

Mary knew me better than anyone. She studied my face and could see right away how important this was to me. "I hope you get this job, too," she said. "I can tell it means a lot to you. I know how unhappy you are with your job."

"I just think I could do something better with my career," I confessed. "I want to be good at my job on purpose. Not just because I got lucky. I want to succeed because I'm the best salesperson I can possibly be. And maybe I can even help my customers in the process." Mary had a way of making me able to say corny things without the slightest bit of self-consciousness.

She stopped correcting her third-grade class's math homework and looked over the rim of her adorable cat-eye eyeglasses. I smiled when I saw the glow in her eyes. "You know why I married you? Aside from your good looks and charm? I married you because you're smart. I know you're going to be a great salesperson. I think you're going to get the job."

"You think I have good looks and charm?"

She laughed. "Figures that's the only thing you heard!"

As she spoke, my cell phone buzzed. My heart raced when I recognized Abe's number. Mary reached for my hand and held it tightly as I took the call. There was still a chance this was Abe calling to say "Thanks, but no thanks."

"Hello?" I said, striving to mask my nervousness. This was the all-or-nothing moment where I would take the leap from job security to career security...which are two very different things.

Job security is what you get when you have a stable company that will employ you indefinitely. Career security is *skills* security. You obtain this kind of security by developing abilities that enable you to achieve results on purpose. Career security travels with you no matter who signs your paycheck. I was about to find out which path I would follow.

"Hello, Adam," Abe said. "I wanted to let you know I've made my decision."

5

Selling From Scratch

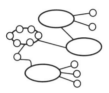

Mary's optimism proved prophetic. I shot her a look of relief and excitement as Abe said in a warm and welcoming voice, "I'd like to offer you the position at Acme."

I accepted on the spot.

Abe asked if I wanted to discuss the decision with my wife. I assured him that I already had. He congratulated me and promised that I would grow tremendously working for him at Acme.

"I'm very excited," I told him. "This is the job I wanted."

"You did better than get a job, Adam. You've made a career leap. Congratulations!"

Little did I know then how right Abe was.

On a brisk autumn morning, my first day at Acme, I rented a car at the Detroit airport and enjoyed a northbound drive up I-75. I sang along with The Who and Led Zeppelin as I listened to classic rock and relished the thought that, Joe's wardrobe aside, some good things had actually come out of the seventies. I arrived in Saginaw, Acme's home office (where Abe was based), in time for lunch. Abe took me to a local dive that offered four different varieties of beef and potatoes or a diet plate that consisted of beef and cottage cheese. We ordered burgers and settled in for what I thought was going to be a getting-to-know-you conversation. But Abe was in no mood for casual chitchat. He got right to business.

"Do you know why I hired you?" he asked.

"You liked my answer about closing the sale," I answered lightheartedly.

"No. I believe you're coachable," Abe said. "I have a system that works. You learned a linear sales process. I'll teach you a different method, one that portrays reality, produces results, and gives you confidence in your career. Try it my way, and you'll get all the latitude and support in the world. If you want to try a different way, I'll support you, but you'll be on a short leash." I was taken aback. Abe's friendly demeanor had given way to a new, more serious style.

Abe said he would shoulder responsibility for the results while expecting me to follow his directions. He assured me that the actions he prescribed would produce the desired results. At Spartan, Joe had only pressured me to achieve results; Abe talked about performance excellence.

Joe never thought I would achieve his outlandish goals; Abe set realistic goals, and expected me to achieve them. Joe rarely observed my activity in the field; Abe planned to inspect my behavior closely. I knew I was facing a new form of accountability.

As we polished off our fries, Abe informed me that I'd spend that afternoon sitting at a desk, prospecting. In the past, I had never been pushed to proactively prospect. Instead, I reactively found sales opportunities by stumbling onto job sites or by using company-provided leads. I was intimidated by the idea of sitting in a room and initiating the *one hundred hours of phone calls* that Abe had alluded to during our interview. I'd thought he was kidding. His expression now indicated he'd been completely serious.

"Don't be nervous," Abe said.

I laughed skittishly, "Well, I am."

"Okay," he said happily. "A little bit nervous can be good." He told me I was ready for the first lesson. Pushing aside his plate, he grabbed a beverage napkin to draw a new diagram. Abe obviously liked to draw pictures.

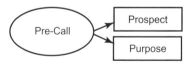

"The time prior to the actual sales meeting is the *pre-call*," he said. "It's the time when you only need to do one thing—*prospect to schedule an appointment*. Of course, before you make the call, you need to create a reason for the appointment. You need a *purpose*. Simple?"

"Simple," I said.

"The only thing I expect you to do this afternoon is start prospecting. I have a secret repository of high-quality leads for you."

"More secrets," I said. "When are you going to tell me *the* secret?" He laughed.

"*The* secret is for later," he said. "My secret repository is...the Internet."

"That's a secret?" I asked.

"Did you use search engines to look up companies to cold-call at Spartan?"

"No. I suppose not."

"Why?"

"Good question." Clearly the Internet was no secret and contained hundreds of leads—really, the only source a salesperson needed. It seemed like such an obvious strategy the moment Abe suggested it. I concluded that salespeople probably thought about it...a lot, but never actually *did* anything about it. Many salespeople tend to procrastinate and find ways to occupy their time rather than proactively invest in a search for new business. Abe would ensure that procrastination was not an option for me.

"I can only assume that, if you never used a free repository containing so much value, then it must be a secret. Otherwise, why didn't you use it?" he asked, clearly amused by his logic. "In any case, it's a very effective tool. I recommend it highly."

To prove I already had a prospecting mindset, I told Abe that Benton Distribution would probably switch to Acme with a phone call. Then I added that I was nervous about prospecting before I received product training.

"Nonsense," Abe said, reaching for a last fry. "You don't need to know anything about the product in order to schedule a few appointments. You'll start learning the product tonight, in your hotel room, by reading through our catalog."

"Homework on the first day?" I asked a little too sarcastically.

He shot me a stern look and ignored my question. "The product is secondary," he assured me. "You need to sell. The product is a tool. Selling is about creating the right relationships and revealing the right fit between client and supplier. That's the job. You need to find some clients."

"But I already have clients at Spartan who I think I can bring over to Acme." I had already contacted Benton, but hesitated before admitting it. For some reason, Abe didn't seem interested.

"You won't need to call those clients," Abe assured me. "Not yet at least."

"What if I can get one of them to come over immediately? Then I wouldn't need to do so much cold-calling." I realized, too late, that I sounded like a teenager whining to a parent as I tried to get out of dish-washing duty.

"Look," Abe said, and for the first time a flicker of impatience crossed his face. "We're on a mission here. The mission is to build your sales skills to the highest level. If I allow you to take the easy path right away, it will deprive you of the opportunity to develop valuable prospecting skills."

"So, you want me to sell from scratch?"

"That's a good way to put it!" Abe said enthusiastically, instantly returning to the exuberant man with whom I had interviewed. "Sell from scratch," he said cheerily. "I like that a lot!"

Selling from scratch meant that I would be trained to create sales opportunities out of thin air—a challenge most salespeople never face. Instead, they're provided existing accounts, leads, or walk-in clients, thus eliminating the pressure to prospect. "Selling from scratch" means you grow a sales territory from zero by generating your own sales leads. It's the only way to achieve career security.

Even though everything Abe had said made sense, I still couldn't get past the *hundred hours* of cold calling. What on earth had I gotten myself into? I hadn't been happy at Spartan, but at least I'd known the ropes. Abe was asking me to perform at a level at which I felt incapable, even if Mary seemed to have so much faith in my abilities.

I suddenly had reservations about my decision to take the job, but it was too late to turn back. I remembered what Joe had said to me when I'd given him my notice. He'd sneered and said, "You'll see how life feels on the other side of the fence. Then you'll know how good you had it here."

I had no intention of giving Joe that satisfaction. I was going to make this work. No matter what it would take.

Abe was true to his word and set me up in a stark cubicle at the corner of an open office. The desk was bare except for a computer and a few pens. He pulled up a chair next to me and produced a leather-bound week-at-a-glance calendar, much like the one I'd noticed in his office during our first interview. Except that this one had my name inscribed on it.

"This is the tool of a sales warrior. It's the only asset you need to achieve career success. All other assets—literature, samples, product knowledge, and the like—are complements. The calendar is your primary sales tool. Fill your calendar with productive meetings and you'll achieve success. Of course, you can use your computer calendar, but there's something about a physical calendar that gives this aspect of the sales process its due weight."

Rather than set the calendar on the desk, Abe held it gently with both hands and presented it with ceremonial significance. I took the calendar, accepting the truth of his conviction, even if I did not yet understand. The fact that he took the time to have my name inscribed made the exchange feel powerfully symbolic. *The calendar is the tool of the sales warrior,* I reminded myself.

Abe indicated I should turn on my computer.

"Search for 'Chicago area builders,'" he directed. When I had a list, he smiled. "Start calling. Take notes as you speak with people." I waited for further instructions, but he gave none.

"But we sell to dealers," I said as Abe stood up. "Shouldn't I be looking for new dealers to sell our product?"

"Not yet. Your value to dealers is your ability to help them sell. Your value in business-to-business selling will always be your ability to help your customers make a profit. You're not selling a window. You're selling a program. Selling is always about offering a service, something intangible. I reiterate: *the product is secondary*."

"How can a product be considered a service?"

"When you buy a house, should the salesperson decide which home to sell you before he understands your needs?" Abe asked.

"Of course not."

"The 'service' provided by the salesperson is helping you find a home that suits your needs and budget. He shouldn't decide which product to offer *prior* to your meeting. The product you end up with is based on his consultation and your specific needs. The salesperson merely provides the service to help you locate the home of your dreams. Correct?"

"Yes."

"Then, it's proven," he said. "Selling is a service and the product is secondary. It's the reason that some real estate agents are top producers and others struggle. They all share the same inventory of houses. The difference between them is the quality of their sales service."

It made sense. "Your service," he added, "is not to sell them our product. Your service is to help them re-sell it. You'll have credibility with your dealers when you can sell to their audience." He smiled. "Now, I want you to call down this list and schedule appointments for Thursday and Friday when we'll be in Chicago together."

"You're going to be in Chicago?" I asked.

"Of course! I promised you that I would do everything in my power to help you succeed. We're starting now. Get to work. Build two solid days of appointments in Chicago. I'll check in with you later this afternoon."

Suddenly, I found myself in basic sales training: the intense, high-pressure exercise required for anyone who wants to excel in sales professionalism. Many—perhaps even most—salespeople never experience the pressure of prospecting from scratch. I'd worked at Spartan for nearly four years without prospecting. Some salespeople go through an entire career without the experience.

My apprenticeship began seconds after Abe left the cubicle. There was no coffee to fetch, no existing customers to call. I had no orders to service, nor had I been given a price list. I had a phone, a list, and a calendar to fill. I was selling from scratch.

Naturally, I procrastinated—first checking my email and then secretly thinking about calling builders I already knew. But there would be no fooling Abe. Then I thought I could just try to get e-mail addresses and contact prospects first in writing. *Nobody is going to answer the phone. How am I supposed to do this?* I thought. *I don't even know anything about Acme's products.* Of course, that wasn't true—I knew enough about Acme and realized that it wasn't necessary to know all the details just to make a few calls. *Don't be a chicken, Adam,* I thought at last. *Just pick up the darn phone.*

I made half a dozen calls without getting an answer. Receptionists blocked my progress on other calls. Each call became more frustrating than the last. Fear became anger, but I persisted. After ten or twelve more fruitless attempts, I heard a bright, "Hello?" I'd been expecting a machine and was taken off-guard.

"Oh! Um... Hi!" I began nervously. "Um, my name is Adam Brody. I'm calling from Acme Windows and wanted to know, um... Could I possibly come in to meet you or maybe the decision-maker... and perhaps tell you, or whoever the decision-maker is, about our products and the great features we have to offer?"

"I'm sure you have a great window," the voice on the other line said coolly. "But I'm good for now. Thanks."

Click.

I angrily crossed off that company. It took five more phone calls before I got through to another receptionist. "Hi! This is Adam Brody calling from Acme Windows.

Is it possible to speak with the person who makes your window purchasing decisions?" I asked.

"It's best to email information," he responded curtly. "Someone will call you if we're interested."

No way, I thought. *I'm getting an appointment.*

"I'm calling because I think we can save you money," I said with rising ire. "Don't you think someone would want to talk to me if they knew we could save you money?"

"I told you," he said, sounding irritated. "You can send information. If our owner is interested, he'll call you."

"So basically you're just trying to get me off the phone, right?" I snapped.

Click. I put my head in my hands.

"How's it going?" Abe asked. I jumped about a foot. He was standing behind me, and I had no idea how long he'd been there. I realized with a sinking feeling that he'd probably heard every word of that last, particularly disastrous call.

"Not so good," I confessed.

"Who were you just speaking with?"

I gave him the name of the builder, but he persisted. "What was the name of the person on the actual line?"

"Oh. I don't know his name."

"He knows who you are," Abe said pointedly. *Right,* I thought miserably. *Adam Brody, the pushy jerk from Acme Windows.* So far, my first day was not exactly going well. I wanted to blame the guy on the call, but I knew the only person I could blame was myself.

"I'm sorry about that call," I said dejectedly. "I probably embarrassed Acme—and myself. I won't let it happen again."

Abe nodded and sat down. "What purpose do you have for your phone calls?"

"What do you mean? I want to sell windows." He waited for me to elaborate, but I had nothing more to offer.

"Adam, your purpose must benefit the client. The promise to provide a lower price is the refuge of the incompetent," he said, more as a philosophical admonition of the profession in general rather than as a criticism of me. "Instead, begin by wanting to help. Tell people you want to learn about their business. Let them know we're a great company but acknowledge that we don't expect to become their supplier overnight. We just want to meet them and learn about them."

That sounded hokey. I told Abe, "There is no way a prospect is going to let me come visit just to ask them questions and learn about them."

He ignored my comment and asked how many people I'd spoken with. I told him that I had a conversation with one decision-maker but was unable to get past the gatekeeper at other offices. He stared at my blank notepad, raising an eyebrow.

"I didn't take notes because I didn't have any real conversations," I protested.

"What was the *name* of that person on the last phone call?"

I got it, but too late. "I don't know. I probably should have found out."

"Maybe," he said with a shrug and let it go at that. "Your choice. But, if you get the name of the person who answers the phone, you have an ally. Then you can address him or her by name the next time you call. Do you see?"

"Yep," I replied. "Easy enough."

He waved me away from the computer screen and pulled up his chair, perusing my list. He picked up the phone and began to dial. After a few seconds, he hung up and told me he'd gotten a voice mail. He calmly repeated the process several times. On his fifth or sixth phone call, he got an answer.

"Good afternoon!" he said, with a genuine smile that was surely felt on the other end of the line. "Abe Isaacson calling from Acme Windows. How are you today?"

He chuckled. "Yep. I *am* doing well and you're right that I'm in a good mood. It's a good way to be, don't you think?" He created energy with his voice. "Who am I speaking with? Teresa, nice to meet you. How can I learn more about your company? I'd like to present our products to the right person there at Crestview Builders."

I watched Abe take notes. He had neatly written *Crestview Builders* on the blank sheet and added Teresa's name beneath it. As he talked, he jotted *Hank Piquell = Owner*. He asked if Hank was in and then waited for a moment. He winked at me.

"Hi, Hank. Abe Isaacson from Acme. How are you? Good to hear. Do you know Acme Windows? Sure, I would expect you to be satisfied with your current supplier and

I have no idea if we would be a fit for you. I'm calling on behalf of my associate, Adam Brody. He covers Chicago. Any chance we could meet you to learn more about your business?"

Hank rejected the idea initially. Abe said, "We're a great company; you're a great company. We don't expect to become your supplier overnight. But at least you'll know we're out here for you." Abe waited, still smiling. "Sure thing!" he said, when Hank had finished talking. "It would be quick. We'd bring some information for your files, but mostly we just want to know how you go to market and build your product. We could stop in briefly this week. How about Thursday? Great!"

Abe added a few more notes after he hung up.

```
┌─────────────────────────────────────────┐
│          CRESTVIEW BUILDERS              │
│                                          │
│  - Teresa — answers phone                │
│  - Hank Piquell = Owner                  │
│  - Builds a few houses per year          │
│  - Custom homes                          │
│  - North shore                           │
│  - Current supplier = Spartan!           │
│  - 2219 Meadow Lane; Barrington          │
└─────────────────────────────────────────┘
```

Abe had made it seem so easy. *He's just lucky*, I initially thought. But deep down, I knew what happened had nothing to do with luck. He looked at me. "What did you learn?"

"You handle people so well. It was a casual conversation."

"Not really," he said. "It was conversational, but hardly a casual conversation. Everything you heard was strategic. Do you understand?"

I nodded sheepishly, knowing I lacked this most fundamental skill of prospecting. He stood and put his hand on my shoulder. "Let's grab a cup of coffee and start again."

We sat in the break room and Abe told me to take notes.

"Step one. Make the person on the phone feel good. A smile can be heard on the other end of the receiver. Get them talking to reduce tension. Ask them who handles purchasing decisions. Got it?"

"Got it," I said.

"Step two," he continued. "Give them a reason for meeting that benefits them. Tell them you want to learn about their business. Sometimes I tell prospects we can just be a convenient alternative. Sometimes I tell them I can provide some marketing ideas that are working for companies like theirs. But always I can figure out how to help them if they give me a chance to understand their business."

I kept writing.

"Step three. Get the appointment. Some salespeople are better when they have a phone script, while others should just have notes. I think you're a note kind of guy, but we'll see. If you struggle, then I suggest you write out a script to get started. You saw me schedule an appointment without a written script, but don't be fooled. I have one." Touching his finger to his temple, he noted, "Right here. It's memorized from years of practice."

"Can I ask a question?"

Abe smiled and said, "Ask many!"

"Why do you say you want to learn about their business?"

Abe considered his words carefully. "Well, because the entire relationship hinges on the business model of your client. Prices are based on volume and your products must adapt to your client's business model or, in the case of a consumer, lifestyle. Those are the superficial reasons.

"The higher level reason is that you can elevate yourself to the status of sales consultant. You want to understand their business to discover opportunities to share market intelligence, a sales idea, suggestions on operational efficiency, and the like. Intelligent businesspeople get this right away, even though most salespeople don't. So I teach this even though I know it won't fully register at the outset. But eventually you'll see the value in slowing the process down to create a high-level business dialogue."

Abe walked me back to my cubicle and sat with me while I made my next few phone calls. A grandmotherly-sounding woman answered on the third one.

"Good afternoon!" I said a bit too energetically.

She laughed. "And good afternoon to you! Who is this?"

"My name is Adam Brody. I work for Acme Windows."

"What can I do for you, Adam?"

"Well," I began. My mind raced as I considered Abe's example and advice. *Keep it conversational*, I thought. Abe smiled as if he could read my mind. "I'm new with Acme. Actually, this is my first day. I'd like to meet a few builders in the area to learn about their businesses."

"Hold on, sweetie," she said. "I'm going to get Fred. Tell him what you told me and you'll be fine."

I took her advice when Fred came on the line, and he kindly asked when I wanted to meet him. "Are you free on Thursday? It wouldn't take too long. I'll be with my boss, if that's okay. I'll just leave some information and ask a few questions."

"Sure, son," he said cheerfully. "Come on by."

Elated, I hung up the phone and wrote a few notes. I'd made an appointment with a builder who seemed genuinely interested in talking. My emotions shifted completely. In the past, I had scheduled meetings with many clients, and I'd met new prospects that contacted our office to speak with a salesperson. But I'd never created a sales opportunity from scratch. Accidental success in the past had produced pleasure. This appointment generated gratification and joy. Abe smiled at my obvious enthusiasm.

"The *purpose*," he explained, "is to understand a prospect and make sure they know you are a valuable resource. Most people don't want to be sold to. They want options. Most importantly, they want to talk about their favorite subject—themselves. Give them the chance and you'll schedule more meetings with ease."

I apologized for failing to get the name of Fred's receptionist. I didn't even learn what kind of house he built.

"What was your goal?" Abe asked.

"I wanted to schedule an appointment."

"And you did. Congratulations! That's the secret."

"*The* secret?"

He smiled enigmatically and stood up. "You'll be fine. Keep going."

The rest of my calls did not go smoothly. I met with repeated rejection and encountered a few rude receptionists. But I avoided conflict, and my stress level diminished. I noted the receptionists' names—even the rude ones—and little bits of information I could glean from each call. I experienced the gratification of putting two additional appointments in my calendar before Abe came to rescue me from burgeoning mental fatigue.

"You're done," he said, when he saw the slump in my shoulders. "No more. There's a moment when you lose it and need to stop. You've reached that moment. It's time for a new task." I had been making phone calls for nearly two and a half hours. My eyes were tired and I was exhausted, but I felt as though I'd accomplished something valuable. I learned more about selling in those two hours than I had in four years at Spartan. I was more excited about work than I'd ever been before.

"You did good," Abe said, and I beamed. "You'll book some more appointments tomorrow. Let's take a walk and let me show you the factory."

Abe spoke casually during our walk, sharing a bit of his personal background. I was surprised to learn that he'd struggled early on in his career, just as I had. He laughed. "Do you think I was born with sales skills?"

I hadn't considered the idea in that way. "No, I suppose not. It probably took some practice."

"A lot," he agreed. "But this is only the beginning."

A thought occurred to me and I shared it. "You still haven't told me the secret."

He smiled. "Nope. Now this window, over here..." As he pointed out the features of Acme's newest product line, I had to bite my tongue. There was something Abe wasn't telling me, something that made him the incredible salesperson that he was. Something, I knew, that could take me from a good salesperson to a great one.

You can dodge me all you like, I thought, as Abe talked. *But I'm going to find out what your secret is.*

6

Aikido Selling

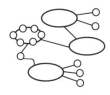

I could barely sleep the night before my big day in the field with Abe. I couldn't bear to disappoint him, especially after he'd watched me flub that terrible phone call on my first day. What if I lost my temper again? What if potential clients canceled their appointments, or just didn't show up? What if my leads were the wrong kind of prospects? What if they just hated me on sight? What if I did something *really* stupid?

Once back in Chicago, I prepared as well as possible. The black paint on my freshly washed Ford Taurus glistened in the morning sun. The dark grey interior floor mats were embossed with angular lines from the vacuum cleaner. The trunk was neatly stocked with product literature and samples. I had printed out our entire route the evening before and highlighted the roads we'd need to take. I even made Mary sit with me while I tried on every sport coat—all three of them—I owned, until she threw up her hands. "They all look fine!" she cried. "You're handsome in all of them! Besides, didn't you tell me this guy doesn't seem to care about clothes?"

I woke early to ensure a timely arrival at Abe's hotel. My palms sweated on the drive to the O'Hare Hilton. When I arrived, he was waiting in the hotel restaurant. He stood and offered me an energetic handshake. A good coach provides a safe environment for the performer, and his cheery disposition did, in fact, lighten my mood. Abe rubbed his hands together. "It's game day!"

I smiled in response to his contagious energy. "Game day?"

"You bet!" he began. "Today we perform. We put on game faces and play our sales roles with no excuses. If you had a bad night, your customers don't care. If you feel pressure at work, they don't want to hear about it. If you're missing the right sales tool during the meeting, too bad. People don't want to hear from you or me today. They want better than you and me!"

"How can we be better than ourselves?" I asked.

"Easy. We play our roles. Your prospects want top-level salesmanship, and that's what they'll get. They're not interested in your hobbies, political views, or personal interests. They want someone who can help them succeed. We're competing with every salesperson the prospect has ever worked with, and we'll be compared to them. So we have to play our roles and play them well."

I had never considered myself an actor playing a sales role, but it made sense. Athletes prepare for competition and, regardless of their moods or challenges off the field, must perform at peak levels on game day. It should be no different for salespeople.

I turned to lead Abe back to my car, but he pointed to a chair next to him instead. "Not yet. Have a cup of coffee. Success is a result of preparation, and I need you to be prepared. We're going to study the skills you need *before* you go into the competition."

I nodded. Abe's expression was focused and intense again.

"The sales call is unlike the pre-call process," he continued. "During the pre-call, you were able to prepare a script, plan your approach for each prospecting call, and take notes without being observed by the client. The sales call is different. Do you remember the 'other stuff' I talked about?"

"Yes! I still have the drawing from the interview," I told him proudly.

"Good. In the heat of the game, you'll be forced to randomly apply those other selling skills." He took out a pad and drew a new diagram.

It illustrated the core skills of the sales call—*building rapport*, *presentation*, *Aikido*, *understanding*, and *the next step*. The names of the skills were changed from his "other stuff" drawing. I recognized he was, true to his word during the interview, holding back some secrets.

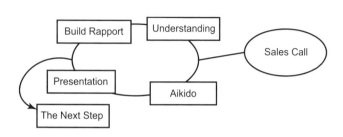

"Understanding?" I asked. "Most people call that 'qualifying' or 'questioning' or 'needs analysis.' Why do you call it 'understanding'?"

"Great question," said Abe. "You told me in your interview that the linear process seemed unrealistic. Yes?"

"Yes, especially the idea of open-ended questions."

"Perfect," he said, his grey eyes gleaming. "It's not about questions. It's about a mindset. Our first objective is to *understand*. We listen and observe. No matter what kind of questions we ask, we must listen in order to understand. We might *read* about prospects in the newspaper or obtain valuable information from our credit department. We *see* what their business looks like and observe the people we meet. We *hear* rumors, which are sometimes valid. Any way we can, using all of our senses, we strive to understand our clients and prospects. You'll be more credible when you first try to understand."

I told him, "Your idea of understanding validates my belief. I think open-ended questions are overrated."

"I agree completely," Abe said. "It's about listening, not necessarily asking. Questions are a tool."

I looked at his drawing again. "I don't know what Aikido is. Is *that* the secret?"

He laughed. "Aikido is a martial art," he informed me. "In Aikido, you use your adversary's momentum to your advantage." He'd gone from laughter to intensity in the space of a breath again. It was part of his charisma, I realized—his uncanny ability to charm in one moment and teach in the next.

"*Adversary* is not a term I like to apply to prospects and clients, but let's build from there. Many traditional sales theories stress power over people and control of situations. They imply that the sales process should always result in outcomes fully within the salesperson's influence. In my opinion, this is not an effective way to sell."

I immediately resisted this concept. "But, if we can't control the situation and results, then what's the point of being salespeople? It's like saying we should just wait to take an order."

"Did I say the salesperson should simply wait?" he asked.

"No. I guess not."

"Do you like to be controlled?"

"No. Nobody does," I responded.

"When you buy a new car, dishwasher, golf clubs, or anything of importance to you, what dictates the timing of your decision?"

"I suppose it's based on need," I said. I realized I had just agreed with him that a salesperson really isn't selling so much as the customer is buying. "But the salesperson can make a big difference and get me to take action," I added defensively.

"Does he *get you to take action*?" he asked.

"He persuades me, yes."

"Forces you to act?"

"No. He can't force me," I said.

"You buy when there is a need. What about golf clubs? Do you own golf clubs?"

"Yes," I said.

"When you last bought a set of golf clubs, what prompted you to act? Did you *need* them?" he asked.

"No," I said. "That's my argument. I didn't need them. The salesperson convinced me to act by showing me how new technology would improve my game. So he really did make the difference."

Abe conceded the point with a lawyerly nod. "Was he the first salesperson you met when you shopped for clubs?" I didn't realize it at the time, but Abe was using the Socratic method on me by cleverly making his arguments through a series of questions that would steer me to certain inevitable conclusions. This method was an effective sales technique that he would later pass on to me.

"Well... no."

"Why didn't you buy from the other one?" he asked.

"Actually, there were two others. The first was pushy and the second didn't seem to know his stuff."

"Keep going," Abe said with excitement. "We're getting somewhere. Keep talking it out."

"What am I talking out?"

"Tell me why you didn't buy from the first two," he prompted. "What did the third salesperson do to convince you?"

I thought back to my purchase. "The third salesperson did something interesting. I remember telling him I didn't like the logo on a set of clubs that he recommended. It was a small thing, but it bugged me. He told me not to buy that set. 'It could affect your game mentally,' he said."

"That's Aikido," Abe said, nodding.

I continued, "I told the salesperson, as he showed a club from another set, that it was way over my budget. He comically spun around to put the club back on the rack without attempting to hand it to me. No argument. No pressure."

"That's Aikido," Abe said again.

"He talked me out of a set I had considered, telling me that I could get as much performance from another set while saving a lot of money. I bought the set he recommended."

"And *that's* Aikido," Abe said. "He helped you make your own decision."

"Exactly," I admitted. "He didn't push at all. I don't like it when—" I stopped. I'd come to the conclusion that proved Abe's argument. He saw my consternation and grinned. He'd let me talk myself into a corner, and I had to admit he was right. I smiled and nodded to acknowledge his victory. "I don't like it when... *salespeople try to manipulate or control me.*"

"Exactly!" Abe beamed. "That's the key. No one does. Aikido avoids conflict and takes the path of least resistance." He poked me gently in the arm and reminded me, "*You* made the decision. *You* determined when the timing was right. The successful salesperson just stayed out of your way to help you see a path."

"Is *that* the secret?"

He gave me an exasperated look. "Let's stick to the point at hand. Aikido is an advanced concept, particularly for beginners. It's hard to believe that less pressure creates better sales results. But you'll discover this truth eventually."

"Every time I buy something," Abe continued, "I instinctively evaluate the sales performance. I dig into my own psychology to understand what motivated me, even if it is vanity or some other reality I must face about myself. My goal is to understand what influences people psychologically."

I thought of the scene in the *Star Wars* series when Yoda drills the young Jedi apprentice, Luke. In that scene, Luke endured a series of frustrating exercises that seemed pointless but that later transformed him into a competent warrior. I enjoyed the thought of Abe as the wise Jedi master training his hotheaded, impetuous apprentice.

At last, Abe seemed to think we'd covered the diagram well enough to get on the road. Our first appointment was at Evergreen Builders, owned by Tom Santa. He'd been curt on the phone, but his level of hostility when we met him in person was nonetheless unexpected. We'd barely sat down across from him before he seized control of the meeting.

"So, Acme Windows, huh?" he began. He didn't offer us coffee, and bypassed any idle conversation. "I did business with you fifteen years ago. If there was anything more that could go wrong with an order, I don't know what the heck it could be. All I can say is that you guys stunk on toast!"

"Well, we—" I started to interrupt, but Abe put his hand on my forearm. I shut up. Tom observed Abe's gesture, looked at me scornfully, and kept right on criticizing. *I should have qualified the prospect better. I should have seen this coming,* I thought frantically. I knew that Abe would be disappointed, and I feared he would soon recognize that, in fact, I did not have the right raw material to succeed in the world of sales.

Tom continued to rant without taking a breath. His order was delayed because of inefficiencies at our office. The windows arrived in the wrong color, a "putrid brown" that he hated. The shipment was incomplete— not that it mattered because the entire order had to be re-manufactured in the correct color. His biggest frustration was the lack of urgency he sensed in the Acme salesperson. He vented for three minutes, which felt like thirty.

I fidgeted. In contrast, Abe serenely projected his concern with a furrowed brow and nods that encouraged

Tom to vent until he had nothing more to say. I was paralyzed with worry when Tom finally ran out of steam and Abe turned to me.

"Where were you fifteen years ago?" he asked me.

I had no idea what he wanted me to say. "Uh... in the seventh grade?"

"See?" Abe said with the perfect level of sarcasm. He leaned back and pointed his thumb at me, "This good-for-nothing didn't lend a bit of help either. I say we take him out back and beat the crap out of him!"

My eyes widened as I turned to face Tom, who scowled at Abe. Abe stared back placidly. The corner of Tom's mouth twitched, and he let out a chuckle that soon turned into a laugh. Abe smiled playfully, and I finally laughed too. Abe took the reins of the meeting by graciously thanking Tom for being so candid.

"I believe you when you say we aren't the company for you," he said. "I'm disappointed that you had such a bad experience. Obviously I'd like to think we're a different company now, and I believe our track record proves we usually get orders right. I'd like to say, on behalf of the entire company, 'We're sorry.' Plus," he concluded with a grin, "If I apologize instead of blaming Adam, I won't have to beat up my new salesperson on his first day in the field. Deal?"

"Deal," Tom said, still snickering. Shortly thereafter we shook hands and left his office. I sensed Tom was embarrassed by his outburst but too prideful to apologize.

"Boy, was that guy mad," I said on the way to the car.

Abe smiled and looked at me as if we were having a casual conversation about nothing. He said, "Let's not sit in front of the office where we can be seen discussing the sales call. Drive away and we can talk."

His reaction triggered an unpleasant flashback. I expected the inevitable reprimand. Would *anything* go right this morning? Fight-or-flight panic filled me as I pulled out of the parking space and headed toward our next scheduled meeting. As soon as we were out of the parking lot, Abe released a huge laugh. I looked over at him, startled.

"That was fun," he said.

"I'm really sorry," I said. I didn't know what else to say.

"Why are you apologizing? You didn't do anything wrong. If anything, I want to apologize to you. I grabbed your arm during the meeting to keep you from interrupting Tom. I didn't want to make you look bad, but more importantly, I didn't want that tense situation to escalate."

I was awed by Abe's comments. Abe was apologizing *to me*? I couldn't believe it. Nevertheless, he did not let a coaching opportunity pass. "I am curious, though. What were you going to say to Tom in the middle of his tirade?"

"I guess I had no plan," I admitted. "But, I felt like I should try to do something to reduce the tension."

"Did you think there was any interruption you *could* make that would reduce the tension?" Abe asked.

After some thought, I concluded, "I suppose not."

"So, what did you learn?"

I pondered his question. "I agree that it's best not to argue. But what did we have to lose? It was like we didn't even try."

"What should we have done?" Abe asked.

"We could have explained we're a different company than the one he dealt with fifteen years ago."

"That's exactly what we *did* do. But rather than make a bold statement out of it, I tried a little humor to illustrate the point. Would you like to know what I saw?"

"Of course."

"First, your observations about the linear process are accurate. You told me the linear process didn't portray reality, and our sales call proved it. There was no *rapport building* at first, and we had little opportunity to *understand* his business. We did manage to make a brief *presentation*. But mostly, we let him vent and express his frustrations. Not very linear."

I nodded. "What do you mean, we didn't build rapport *at first*?"

"The linear process tells you that building rapport is a single event, but that's not true. Think about the word *building*. You're creating something, and that takes time. Your rapport with each client will continually evolve. We built rapport by injecting humor later in the meeting. That put the situation in perspective and also reminded him that you're a real person."

"That was very clever," I said. "I don't know if I'm going to be able to do stuff like that."

"It takes time. You'll develop the skill," Abe said. "Taking a non-linear approach allows us to deal with each situation as it arises. Tom was too angry for us to learn much about his business today, but I wasn't thrown because I don't expect to be able to follow a single set pattern in a sales call."

"I guess there's no way we could have alleviated his hostility."

"But we did," Abe countered.

"How so?" I asked. I was trying to listen while concentrating on the directions to our next sales call. The intensity of the morning was heating up.

"We didn't argue," he said. "We didn't make a product presentation. We didn't try to ask him questions about his business or suppliers. We simply listened and accepted his comments. We thanked him for his candor. What more could we do? He was being honest and may truly have had a horrible experience. So why argue?"

"Right," I agreed. "We couldn't win."

"Welcome to Aikido selling," Abe said. "When the opponent throws a punch, you can block it and you will both get hurt. Or you can evade it and allow the momentum of your adversary to take him off balance."

"I think I saw that," I asserted. "That happened with Tom."

"When?" Abe asked. I realized he was testing me.

"Tom seemed embarrassed by his outburst," I said slowly, anxious to find the right answer. "He certainly wasn't apologetic. But he wasn't proud of treating us harshly either. I think he was surprised by your response and the fact that you didn't argue with him. When you said you believed him, that we 'weren't the company for him,' I thought he leaned in toward you as if urging us not to give up too quickly."

"Very good," Abe said. "I sensed the same feeling. *That* is Aikido selling. He may never do business with Acme again. Life is too short to convince someone against his will. If you argue with anyone, they naturally become more defensive. On the other hand, if you let them have their say, people express their emotions and eventually calm down. You'll discover that some of them even apologize for their anger. This concept will serve you well in all aspects of selling and, in many ways, dealing with life challenges."

"But we never really tried to sell him. You didn't tell him about our products or services," I said.

"So talking is selling?" Abe asked.

"I just meant that you didn't make a presentation."

"So making a presentation is selling?"

Driving and having this intense conversation at the same time was grueling. I was terrified I'd miss the next turn. But I realized where the conversation was headed. "No," I admitted. "Selling is listening and talking both."

"I *was* selling," Abe stated unequivocally. "Don't doubt that for a second. I promise you that nothing I do in a sales meeting is without strategy. Whenever I'm with a prospect or customer, I am always selling. That's what you do on game day."

Abe continued, "I told Tom we're a different company than we were fifteen years ago, which *is* a presentation. I wanted him to realize that he can reconsider his opinion of us. Not all presentations are about products and service.

Presentations should inspire changes in perspective. The presentation goal is to educate, inspire, and clarify expectations."

I nodded.

"You might want to call Tom in two weeks if you haven't heard from him," Abe suggested. "Thank him for his time and reiterate our apologies for his past experience. Then leave it at that. He might surprise you. Or he might not. But it's the nice thing to do."

I weighed Abe's words. I had nothing to lose. "Of course I'll call him," I said. "But do you really think it will do any good?"

"Sometimes people surprise you," was all Abe said.

After that, we drove in silence for a while. I'd managed to not get lost while going over the sales call with Abe. I contemplated what I'd learned, thinking yet again how Abe seemed to have all the answers. Suddenly, a thought occurred to me.

"What's the *next step*? You wrote that down on the sheet. But you didn't say what the next step is."

"It's the secret," Abe said matter-of-factly.

"Why is it a secret?" I asked.

Abe chuckled and said, "It's not *a* secret. It's *the* secret."

"Ok, then. What's *theeee* secret?" I asked.

"*The* secret must remain a secret for now."

"Are we Laurel and Hardy?"

He laughed. "You mean Abbot and Costello."

He even knew the "Who's on First?" routine better than I did. But he still hadn't answered my question. *He's not going to keep his secret for long,* I thought. I was going to get it out of him. "What is the secret? Is the next step the secret?"

"Yes," Abe said. "The next step is the secret to closing the sale."

He looked out the window, but not before I saw a huge, impish smile spread across his face.

"Did you hear that guy say we stunk on toast?" he asked.

I laughed. "I *did* hear that."

"What in the world does 'stunk on toast' even mean?"

I grinned. "I have no clue, but I wouldn't have it for lunch."

Abe laughed hard. The day was becoming fun again.

"Abe?"

"Yes, Adam?"

"I'm not sure I understand the secret."

He smiled. "You will. Trust me."

I hoped he was right.

7

Sales Reality

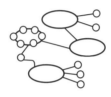

We drove to see Hank Piquell in Barrington, an old suburb of Chicago with new money. Large houses, finished in assorted colors of earth-tone bricks and set on two-acre lots of perfectly manicured lawns, dotted the landscape. Each home represented a different variation of the modern Georgian facade with expansive hip roofs that stretched to the clouds. We pulled up to the address of Crestview Builders.

"It looks like a home rather than an office," I said, stopping short of the driveway.

"It looks like a *nice* home," Abe said, indicating that I should pull in.

"Should we go there?"

"Sure. Lots of builders work from their homes. Remember that *understanding* is more than asking. We also observe. If we are calling on someone who builds homes like this one, it could be a good lead, right?"

"Yes! If he builds houses like this!"

"When two salespeople make a joint call, only one should be in the lead," Abe said as I unbuckled my seatbelt. "It's distracting to a client when two salespeople interrupt each other. It also diminishes the effectiveness of the sales call. I'd like to take the lead on this next call, okay?"

"Sure," I answered, pleased to be able to observe on this round.

"Great. I'll be in the lead then as we work towards the next step. I'll try to get us there."

"What's the next step?"

"It's the secret," Abe said, chuckling.

"Funny," I said, as I grabbed my notepad and some product literature. "I get it... but what *is* the next step?"

Abe grew serious again. "At this point, we don't know. We hope it's a follow-up meeting. That's the goal. Some prospects want to talk; others want to jettison you out of their office quickly. Before we can assume anything, we need to understand Crestview Builders' business model. If they seem like a good lead, we hope to create another meeting."

"Our goal for meeting is another meeting?"

Abe nodded. "That sums it up. Let's go."

We rang the bell adjacent to the large mahogany door. A tall, slender, fortyish blond woman, dressed in jeans and a light-blue collared shirt, answered. She smiled and looked at us with piercing green eyes. I figured we were at the wrong house until she asked, "Are you with Acme?"

"We are," Abe said confidently.

"I'm Teresa, Hank's wife," she said, stepping back and inviting us in with a gesture. "Hank," she called, "the Acme salespeople are here." Then she offered us coffee, which Abe accepted. I was too nervous, so I passed.

Hank walked straight towards us from the kitchen and extended his hand. He was tall and tanned, with dark brown hair starting to grey at the temples. He and Teresa made a strikingly handsome couple. We followed Hank into his office, which was located just to the right of the foyer.

The office was adorned with mahogany wainscoting that reached halfway up the walls. The credenza behind Hank was filled with plaques, business books, photos of teenaged children as handsome as their parents, and some small golf statues. My instinct was to ask him about the golf statues, but I remained silent so Abe could run the meeting. I was a bundle of nervous energy, and my thoughts were so loud in my head that I felt sure Hank could hear them.

"Gentlemen, thank you for stopping by. Any trouble finding the place?" Hank asked.

Abe looked at me and waited. "Not at all," I said hastily. "You gave Abe perfect directions. Thanks for having us. Your office is beautiful. I see you golf."

"I do," Hank said.

"I'm a big-time golfer," I said. I shared my opinions on the top courses in the area, my passion for the sport, and the lessons I had been taking. I carried on. Abe was smiling and listening as if he hung on every word, but I had a sudden feeling he wasn't happy with me. Hank was nodding politely, but his eyes kept flicking back to Abe. Teresa brought Abe his coffee.

"I think we spoke on the phone," Abe said to her, smoothly cutting off my glowing review of yet another local course.

"We did. You're the guy who's having fun," she said.

"Always," he said. "Otherwise, what's the point?"

"Indeed," she said happily. "I'll leave you three to your business."

Hank laughed. "I love it when she acts like the doting wife. Teresa does the books around here and is a licensed real estate agent. She's the other half of our business. Anyway, what can I do for the two of you?"

The question threw me off—a potential client asking what he could do for *us* rather than the other way around. I would have immediately presented our product literature and started talking. But Abe took a different approach.

"Nothing that I know of," he said. "We're here to see what we can do for you! Mind if we ask a few questions about your business?"

"I'd be disappointed if you didn't," Hank said. "What do you want to know?"

Abe shrugged and turned up the palms of his hands. "Please tell us what we *should* know."

Hank smiled and explained that he had built the home we were in and several similar homes in the area. His home was originally intended as a model. "But the space is perfect for my office, and I have the conference table for meetings. I like the workspace too. Teresa decided the house was perfect for the rest of the family too, so we moved in. We love it here, and the school district is great for our kids."

"How many do you have?" Abe asked.

"Two. Jason is fifteen, in his first year of high school. It looks like he'll make the varsity golf team, which we're thrilled about. Lisa is twelve and has a great group of friends. Teresa tells me this is our last home. We're here for the long haul."

"Wonderful," Abe said. "And business is good?"

"Knock on wood," Hank said. "We've built three this year and have two in the ground. We've got some nice prospects brewing for the coming year as well."

I wanted to jump on the opportunity to price his upcoming projects, but Abe waited for more information. I was about ready to leap out of my chair. Abe sat quietly, hands folded in his lap and legs crossed. Hank stopped talking.

"How do you get your new clients?" Abe asked.

"All of our work is custom. We have symbiotic relationships with two architects in the suburbs on the North Shore off Lake Michigan. They refer clients our way. Sometimes clients come to us and we refer them to the architects. We collaborate to create win–win situations for everyone involved. Naturally, I like it when clients come to me first," Hank concluded with a wink.

"Gives you more control?" Abe asked.

"Definitely! It allows us to use products we prefer, although we usually favor the same products as the architects in our network. It all works out nicely."

Abe asked about Hank's operational practices, and Hank described how he managed scheduling, subcontractors, and land acquisition. It was a lesson in business for me. The process of selling and building a custom home fascinated me. I was even more captivated by the amount of information Abe was obtaining from a single meeting. He shifted the dialogue from Hank's business practices to product purchasing. "If you don't mind me asking, which window products do you typically choose?"

I was relieved. Hank was a strong prospect, and I'd been wondering when Abe would get to the subject that mattered most.

"As I told you on the phone," Hank said, "we've been working with Spartan and have had no problems with the product. They have service and delivery issues, though. That being said, I'm not ready to throw them out the window." Hank laughed at his bad joke. "But I do want to explore some alternatives."

Abe asked me to hand him the literature, which I did excitedly, thinking that I'd finally see a master salesperson present his product. Instead, Abe handed the literature across the desk without comment. *What the heck is he doing?* I wondered. *Is he seriously going to blow this opportunity?* Hank casually scanned the catalog.

"What sort of service problems?" Abe asked.

Hank looked up. "Let's say personality problems and leave it at that."

Abe nodded. "What do you know about Acme?"

"I hear good things. Do you know the builder Steve Victor?"

"Sure do," Abe replied. "I worked with Steve on several of his projects when I was the salesperson in this area."

It was astounding to me that both knew the same builder. I concluded it was all a setup. "Have you two met before?!" I asked suspiciously. Both men looked at me, Abe more stunned than Hank. It was the first time I saw Abe look flustered, and I realized I had interrupted his sales momentum.

"I don't think so," Hank said, noticing the error of a rookie salesperson. He had too much class to be rude and smiled at Abe, "Have we met before?"

"Not that I know of," Abe said, before adding with a bold pronouncement to a non-existent audience: "Ladies and gentlemen, for my next trick, let the record show that Hank and I have never met. Now I'm going to ask him to pull a card from the deck..."

Hank laughed. I smiled sheepishly. Abe chuckled and then shifted emotionally to regain power and leadership of the situation.

He said in a sincere, soft tone. "Steve will tell you that the Acme brand helps him create credibility for his homes. People know Acme in this market. Our windows are a way for builders to distinguish their homes."

Hank continued thumbing through the literature. "Where are these made?" he asked.

"Saginaw, Michigan," Abe said.

"Seems like a long way to come for a window sale," Hank said. "How can you service a market from such a long distance?"

"We don't sell directly to builders," Abe explained. "We have a great network of dealers and salespeople that we can refer you to. I believe Steve buys from Classic. They're one of our best."

"Oh. I can't buy from you?"

"No, you wouldn't want to," Abe said. "Like you just said, it's a long way to go to manage a relationship."

"I'd like to find a way to cut out the middle man," Hank said, but Abe only smiled. Hank was quiet for a moment. My heart was racing, but Abe didn't break the silence. Finally, Hank said, "I'll tell you what. I'll have some blueprints available in two weeks. If you want, you can pick up a set and shoot me a price. No promises. I'm not sure I'm done with Spartan yet, but at least I'd see where you guys stack up price-wise."

"Fair enough," Abe said. "We usually aren't less expensive. But there are some features that justify the added investment and increase your profits."

Hank nodded thoughtfully. Abe said, "Let us get out of your hair so you can get some work done. How about if Adam calls you late next week to set up a time to pick up the blueprints?"

"Good," Hank said, as he rose and walked around his desk. He shook our hands. "Adam, it was good to meet you. Thanks for your time. Abe, I really appreciate you coming from the home office to meet a small builder like me."

"Thank you," I said enthusiastically. Hank was a gentleman.

"Thank you," Abe said. "And thank Teresa for the coffee, please."

I walked to the car with mixed feelings. On one hand, I was ecstatic that the meeting had gone so well. On the other, I was sure I'd embarrassed myself again in front of Abe with my impatience and visible anxiety.

As we drove off, Abe asked me when I would stop to take my notes.

"Which notes?"

"*The* notes," Abe said. "You think you'll remember the content of this conversation a week from now, but you won't. You need to jot down how many houses Hank builds per year; that Teresa sells his homes; why he's considering a new supplier; where he gets his leads; and so forth. I wanted to ask about the architects in his network for referral opportunities, but the timing was wrong. It's worth jotting down a reminder to ask for those referrals in the future. Make sense?"

"Makes sense," I said, as we wound our way along the residential streets towards I-90. "Would it be okay if I pulled over?"

"I recommend it," Abe said.

I soon filled half a page with neatly organized bullet points.

Abe sat silently, looking forward, in the passenger seat while I wrote. When I was done, I looked at Abe and said, "I'm sorry for what I said during the meeting."

"You mean for thinking Hank and I had previously met? Forget it," Abe said with a wave of his hand, before adding, "But I wouldn't make it a habit of challenging your teammates on joint sales calls."

"Point taken," I said.

"Other than doubting Hank and I were strangers to each other, how do you think the sales call went?" Abe asked.

We remained parked. "Well, it's a great lead!" I said. "I'm excited about the opportunity."

"Yes, it's a great lead. I agree. But my question is about the *sales call*—the performance."

I didn't understand the difference. He clarified, "Sometimes you have a great sales opportunity but make a bad sales call. Sometimes you have a mediocre lead but make a great sales call. Let's not talk about the quality of the lead yet. Let's talk about the sales performance. You can succeed by accident or on purpose. Let's try for 'on purpose.'"

Abe was telling me nearly the exact same thing my golf instructor had told me months ago. *Success on purpose,* I thought, remembering how important that phrase was to me. "I was amazed at the amount of information you got from him. That was really impressive."

"Thank you, Adam. Tell me how it happened."

I replayed the conversation. "The sales call, in this case, was actually linear. We *built rapport* with small talk. Then you asked questions to *understand* his business. Then you made a *presentation*. Then you suggested *the next step*."

"Very good," Abe said with a smile. "Perfect. But there was also an objection—some time for *Aikido*. Do you remember?"

"Yes," I said. "Hank asked us if our prices were competitive."

"No," Abe said with a shake of his head. "That was the beginning of a possible negotiation, not an objection. The objection was his request to buy from us directly. Do you recall?"

"Oh! Yes. You told him it wouldn't be in his best interests. But I don't see how that's Aikido. You disagreed with him."

"I explained our inability in terms of *his best interests*. We won't cut out our middleman. But the fact is, we wouldn't do a good job delivering small quantities from three-hundred fifty miles away."

I saw his point. "It's good when you can make the sales call go in linear order, right?"

"Yes. Very good. It gives you a sense of control and enables you to manage the sales process more effectively. It's usually a sign that you have a cooperative prospect, too," Abe said. "Your analysis was excellent, Adam. Now, grab your calendar."

It was in my briefcase, sitting on the back seat. Abe could see that all our meetings for the day were entered.

"Always take your calendar into meetings. If you get a chance to make a follow-up appointment during the meeting, you'll need your calendar. It's part of the secret."

I nodded.

He suggested that I make a note to call Hank next week. He said he always put his follow-up list on the Sunday page of his calendar; that gave him a quick reference guide for his weekly follow-up tasks. It made sense, although he allowed that I'd work out my own system over time.

Next, Abe took a piece of paper from his notebook and drew another picture. He was back in teaching mode, and I paid careful attention.

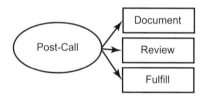

"The sales call is over, but it's not complete until you've taken care of business after the meeting. I call it the *post-call*," he explained. "It's the other linear part of selling. You regain control and no longer have the burden of pressure that exists during the sales call. First, *document* so you can remember key information later. You can either forget crucial details, or impress clients with your incredible memory. The difference is in documentation.

"Next, *review* the meeting. Be sure to focus on the performance, not an evaluation of the prospect. Ask yourself what you *did well* and what you *could do better*.

You perfectly described what went well when you said the meeting flowed as we would like. Sales calls don't always happen in a linear progression, but it's nice when they do."

I listened intently as Abe continued.

"By isolating each skill, you can recognize what went well and where you can improve. Let me share my thoughts so you can learn. Okay?" Abe didn't wait for an answer. "The meeting started out well, but we lost some momentum early on. Do you remember when?"

"No," I admitted.

"Do you remember talking about golf?"

"Yes," I said. "I was trying to break the ice. I thought that would be okay."

"Breaking the ice is good, but whose golf game were you talking about?"

I paused. I'd been talking about myself the whole time. "But," I protested, "Hank and I both golf. He seemed interested in hearing about the golf courses I discussed, right?"

"You hope," Abe corrected. "His only interest in golf might be his teenage son's talents. Or Hank might be a former pro golfer. Or he and his wife might love golfing as a means to spend time together outside of work. The truth is that we don't know. You were probably trying to make *yourself* comfortable in the uncomfortable environment of his home. Is that possible?"

"No," I said, fooling only myself. Abe shot me a look. "Well... okay. Yes. I was uncomfortable and wanted to ease the tension," I added.

"There was no tension for me. Do you think Hank was tense?"

"No. I guess the only tense person was me," I said. Well, that confirmed it. I *had* embarrassed myself in front of Abe.

But Abe didn't chastise me. "If you feel tense, relax by breathing air into the back of your lungs. Talking about yourself only increases tension. It shows disrespect for the client's time. When I started out in sales, my mind was always busy. I've since learned to calm my mind, and you will too. It's an Aikido thing. Remember that the purpose of *building rapport* is to make your clients and prospects comfortable. Right?"

"Yes, sir," I said.

"Good," he said. "Next we listened to *understand*, and that went extremely well. The fact that you doubted Hank and I were perfect strangers proves a point. You were surprised by the amount of information we acquired, correct?"

"I was amazed!" I said.

"That's the power of good listening. People will open up more than you expect. Notice that I first gained information about his business. Why? I want to learn about the ways in which our clients sell *their* products. Our clients don't make and build things for a living. They sell them. So work to understand how your customers sell things. Okay?"

"Yes. It makes sense." I thought back to my days at Spartan. Everything Abe was saying resonated with the feelings I'd had at the time. Listening was the key, not some arbitrary myth about the one single right way to understand your client.

"Good," Abe said, continuing his lecture. "Notice I asked who he purchases from *after* we understood a bit about his business. He opened up, probably because we had taken a sincere interest in him. On the phone, he said everything was fine with Spartan. During the meeting, he sang a different tune. He didn't share the reasons why he is unhappy. But that's okay. It's a sign that we have a good opportunity.

"Finally, I asked him what he knew about Acme *before* making a presentation. Much to my pleasure, he knew a builder with whom I've had great success. That was just dumb luck, which of course happens when you work hard. If anything, we should be wondering why I haven't met Hank sooner. I should have asked Steve Victor for referrals and met Hank long ago. Do you see?"

"Well, I guess so," I said. "But that's being pretty hard on yourself. You're a great salesperson."

"Of course I'm being hard on myself," Abe said. "If I can't take criticism from myself, then who can I learn from? I think I'm a good salesperson. But in this case, I have to remind myself that the learning moment is to ask for more referrals in the future. Who is going to judge *your* performance when we're not together?"

I think he wanted me to say, "Me." So I did.

"Yes! Exactly. That's why you *review* your performance. It's the only way to learn and grow."

I wanted to criticize Abe's presentation but knew to be careful. "Abe, I was surprised by your presentation. You didn't highlight the features and benefits of our products."

Abe grinned. "I didn't?"

"Well, we have a lot to offer," I said. "The quality of manufacturing is awesome, and there are a lot of product features and options that make us better than the competition."

Abe laughed. "How long could we have gone on talking about our products, options, performance ratings, deliveries, people, service, and the remaining details of our company if we were given as much time as we wanted?"

"Hours?"

"Exactly. Which part of that presentation should I have added?"

I thought about the things I might have said. "I'm not sure. I'm only saying that we didn't talk about the product at all."

"What was our goal before the meeting?"

"Our goal was the *next step*."

"Good," Abe said. "During the meeting, what became our next step?"

I'd just made the note in my calendar. "Schedule a meeting to get the blueprints."

"Excellent! Then the presentation was fine. We accomplished our goal. What will your next step be at the *next* meeting?" I was puzzled. Abe added, "It's not a trick question."

"Oh! I'll get the blueprints."

"Excellent. That is *fulfillment*. You will fulfill your promise. You will then strive to understand his expectations. You'll make it your goal to get him talking about the blueprints, ironing out the product and scheduling details. You will not overpromise. You will provide a realistic time frame to get a price proposal to him. You will sweat the details so that no mistakes will occur if he gives you the order. You won't give a random range of weeks to place an order. You'll take control by telling him when he needs to give you the order if he wants his product on time. That is how you'll fulfill his long-term expectations. Right?"

I nodded.

"You have a future *next step*, which is to get referrals to his architects. Then you'll call those architects and schedule meetings with them. Your *next steps* include a phone call, a meeting to pick up blueprints, getting names, scheduling meetings with architects, and, later, delivering a price proposal for his next job. Do you see?"

It was making sense. "Yes, sir!"

"Welcome to the secret. Let's drive to our next meeting. We're on a roll!"

"*This* is the sales secret?" I asked.

"Yes. You're living the sales secret," Abe said.

"I don't think I quite get it. Which part is the secret?"

"Don't worry. It's better to know and think you don't than to not know and think you do. You already know. You just don't know you know."

Now *that* was worthy of Yoda. "Huh?"

Abe giggled. I sighed, renewing my determination. I *would* get the secret out of Abe. No matter how inscrutable he got.

8

Game Time Chatter

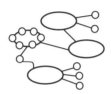

Adrive across my Chicago sales territory took five or six hours at the wrong time of day. I had set up our appointments to minimize travel time but nevertheless got stuck in traffic. Abe used the time to speak about selling and solicited my opinions.

In the past, my conversations with co-workers focused on families, hobbies, and the latest news. We discussed baseball a lot, frequently engaging in debates of the relative merits of the White Sox and the Cubs. These debates were ridiculous, since both teams had set records for futility by lasting decades without a championship between them.

My dialogue with Abe was different. As we drove, I chattered about the last baseball game I'd seen and a particularly awful play I couldn't believe the Cubs had flubbed. I was really building up steam when he interrupted me. "Do you know what baseball players talk about between innings?"

"The girls in the stands?" I happily suggested.

"No, Adam. No," he said, gently correcting me. "They talk about baseball. The hitters talk about the pitchers' strengths and weaknesses. The pitchers talk about ways to exploit hitters' vulnerabilities, such as who can't lay off the curveball."

I nodded. *So what?* I thought. *I'm talking about baseball, too.*

"Do you know what salespeople talk about between sales calls?" he asked, as if reading my mind.

"Baseball!"

"Yes! Exactly!" he said. "They talk about baseball. Do you know what *great* salespeople talk about?"

Oh, right. Even I could see where he was going with this one. "Selling?"

"That's correct, Adam," Abe said. "During game day you keep learning. The difference between selling and baseball is that the game *is* our practice. We have to be more attentive than a professional athlete on game day because we don't have the luxury of practice days in the field. This is our practice and game at the same time. That's why we review every sales call."

When Abe interviewed me, I'd told him about my commitment to growth as a salesperson. Abe was holding me accountable to that commitment. *This is what you wanted, Adam,* I thought. Sure, it would have been easier to spend the rest of the drive ranting about the Cubs. But

I was here to learn. Suddenly, I felt more like an adult than I ever had before.

Soon enough, we arrived at the model home of a tract builder. Abe said, "You're in the lead."

"I think it would be better if you led."

"Better for whom?" he asked. I sighed again. He'd just won that round before I'd even gotten all the way in the ring. *He sees right through me,* I thought. *Of course he knows that I'm just scared. I guess it's now or never.*

We walked into a modestly appointed model home. The furnishings looked cheap and the décor was a uniform beige, from the industrial carpeting to the undecorated walls. The house was small, and the building materials and interior were generic and low-priced—including the windows. *Next time, a little more research, Adam,* I thought. I hoped I hadn't blown this call before it even started. We met with the superintendent in charge of the subdivision and discovered he was a part-time farmer.

The sales call went better than I'd expected, though. Well aware that Abe was watching my every move, I jumped immediately into a product presentation. I pointed out the custom features of Acme's high-end line of wooden windows.

"I don't know," the superintendent said, picking up one of my brochures without opening it. "We don't really do custom work. All our windows are aluminum, and pretty inexpensive."

Since that was a low-priced category in which we were not willing to compete, I pressed the issue of our more expensive wood windows, which were usually used in luxurious homes. "You can sell the benefits of our product to your customers," I suggested, pleased with my response. He couldn't argue with that—and neither could Abe.

Yet something nagged at me. I felt like I was "selling" but not really accomplishing much.

"Thanks for stopping by, gentlemen," he said. "I'd better get back to work." And that was the end of our visit.

As we drove away, Abe asked, "When you prospect for gold, what are you looking for?"

The answer seemed obvious. "Gold."

"Good. Yes! Gold. Do you think that was a golden lead?"

I thought about the meeting. I'd done a fantastic job of presenting our products—even Abe couldn't argue with that. But there was no getting around the fact that the builder had no use for them. I sighed. Again. "Well, no. Not really."

"Then don't push. Remember Aikido? The two biggest mistakes salespeople make are pushing the wrong client or pushing at the wrong time. This was the wrong client. We want prospects who are legitimate candidates to buy our products. Make sense?"

"It does," I admitted. "But I figured..."

"But. But. But. Get your 'but' out of the way!" Abe said with a laugh. "That wasn't a great lead. It might be someday, but not today. We might produce a cheap product that competes in the future, although I doubt it. Or the builder might start building a category of homes that fits our product. So, remember those index cards? You can create a list of prospects and enter that builder's information. Make a follow-up call six months down the road."

"Yes," I said. The index cards were Abe's version of a database. I didn't tell him I would be putting my contacts into a computer software program. But I did get his point. I nodded, entering notes into my calendar.

"So, how did the sales call go?" Abe asked.

"Not too well," I admitted.

"Why?"

"Well, it's not really a very good lead."

"Was that my question?"

I remembered how we'd reviewed the last sales call. "No. The lead is a bad lead. But the sales call went well, and I felt my presentation was good. We can have a good call to a bad prospect."

Abe countered, "Or we can have a bad sales call to a bad prospect. That was a bad call. It was not a great performance."

"But—" I protested. Abe put up a hand.

"No defense. No apologies. We're on the same team. We're learning. Let's maximize our learning. Okay?"

"Okay," I said grudgingly.

"Good. Relax. You did okay. But you're so much better than okay. You have the potential to be a great sales performer." Trust Abe to make a reprimand sound like a compliment! His praise only made me want to work harder. "But your performance on this sales call was not up to potential. We're not talking about the *performer*; we're talking about the *performance*.

"The initial greeting was fine, and I really enjoyed the way you let him talk about his corn farm. You probably had nothing to add to the conversation, so you listened to his viewpoint on a very personal subject. Make sure you do that intentionally in the future. Assume you don't golf the next time your client talks about *his* golf game. Make sense?"

"Got it."

"Good. People don't care how much you know until they know how much you care. Your *understanding* of this call was mediocre, Adam. You focused exclusively on the product they purchase, and you learned they use aluminum windows. You don't know, however, how they market their homes or manage their construction. We met with a mid-level manager who seems involved, but we don't know who else is involved in decision-making leadership roles. They seem busy building houses, but we don't even know how many. Right?"

I nodded, my heart sinking and my earlier bravado evaporating. *Wow.* I'd really screwed up.

"There is a lot more you didn't find out. Even though we probably won't sell our products to this prospect, you need to develop the skill of *understanding*. There's always the possibility that this client builds another type of home that could use our product. I happen to know that's not the case here, but *you* need to know from your own investigation. Had this been a valuable lead, you would have reduced yourself to a price salesperson. You need to understand their business because prospects open up when you show your interest. We don't try to learn about their business in order to manipulate them. The key is to *understand* because you genuinely want to help other people succeed. Do you see?"

The thing was, I *did* see. What Abe was saying was that my job wasn't just to sell things. My job was to meet a potential client's needs, to care about the client's best interests as much as my own. If I cared about the same things the client cared about, we could only help each other. On the call with Hank, Abe's interest had been genuine. Abe had really listened, and Hank had responded to his interest. *I have to develop my listening skills to truly grow in this job*, I thought. *And I need to keep my focus on* helping the client*, not just selling our product.*

"Yes, sir," I said in response to Abe's question. He was watching me closely. I wondered if he could see how his lessons were transforming my sales mindset.

"Good," he said. "Finally, your presentation was completely off target. You violated the theory of Aikido selling by pushing him to use a product that would render the builder uncompetitive. Not only would the timing be wrong, the use of our product would be wrong. We're not a fit. Do you understand?"

"Yes, but—" I said. Abe raised one eyebrow. "I mean, what could I have done differently? What presentation could I have made?"

"Great question!" Abe said. "When you stop defending, you start thinking. What presentation could you have made?"

"I just asked you that!" I said.

"I just asked *you* that."

I laughed. Abe's eyes glowed with wisdom and kindness. I knew he would help me find the right answer, and I knew he wouldn't judge me—even if it took me all day. "I could have said we're probably not the window for him..." I trailed off. I had no idea what else I could have said.

"Perfect," Abe said. "That's exactly what I would've said. We're probably not the window company for him at this time. I would have told him we make a window for a different type of home and he would have recognized the truth in that. He may have suggested a different builder for us to call or told us that his company has a different division we could visit—or he might have just thanked us for our time and sent us on our way. Remember the first golf club salesperson who pushed you?"

"Yep. I see. I was just like him, pushing the product I wanted to sell, rather than the product the client needed."

"Make no mistake," Abe said. "Telling him 'we're not the company for you' *is* a presentation. It establishes credibility. It avoids conflict. It's Aikido selling. Make sense?"

I nodded. Joe would have pushed me to sell to this builder, no matter how unwanted my product was, but Abe faced reality. He taught me to prospect for a better lead when I ran into an unqualified one.

"Well done," Abe said.

"What was well done?" I asked. "I failed miserably."

"Do   you   agree   that   you   need   to   work   on *understanding*?"

"Yes. I do."

"Good," Abe said. "Well done. Next stop?"

I asked, "Are you asking me what the next step is with that builder?"

"No," Abe said. "Where is our next *stop*?"

"Who's on first?"

"Exactly."

I groaned aloud.

9

Peer to Peer

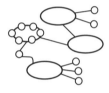

Our next stop was an after-lunch meeting at Deardon Homes, the office of Fred Deardon. The dimly-lit office was paneled in dark brown wood. It was filled with worn, sharply-angled furniture, glass coffee tables, and fabrics in muted brown tones that would have been more stylish a few decades prior. A woman in her sixties sat at a wooden desk. She wore too much blue eye shadow, and her grey hair was perfectly coiffed in a beehive that seemed to match the age of the furnishings. Her dark grey suit and white silk blouse completed an authoritative image that belied her friendly demeanor.

"What can I do for you, gentlemen?" she asked in a raspy smoker's voice that I recognized. She was the woman who had called me "Sweetie" on the phone.

"Hi, I'm Adam Brody, and I have an appointment with Fred," I said way too formally.

She and Abe exchanged smiles. "I'm Abe. I'm his caddy," he said with a nod in my direction.

She laughed and said, "I'm Joyce. Fred's expecting you. I'll get you something to drink if you'd like."

Abe accepted coffee, even though he'd had three cups during lunch. Joyce warmed to him immediately, and they bantered a bit before Abe and I went in to meet with Fred. The meeting was brief. I tried to remember everything Abe and I had gone over in the car. *Don't screw this one up!* I thought. *Show Abe you're learning.*

After we completed the sales call with Fred Deardon, Abe asked me to review it.

"Well," I began, still seated in the car, "the introduction with Fred went well. He's stiff and I don't think he really wanted a lot of small talk. I noticed that his office is impeccable and he's organized. We didn't find out for sure, but I got the sense that Joyce has worked for him for a long time. I was glad that I asked him 'Can you tell us about your business?' because..." I paused to think. "Well, I didn't know what else to ask. I like the way you did that with Hank, and I figured I should do the same with Fred. And the amount of information he shared surprised me. Although his office seemed so old that I first thought he was getting ready to retire, the complete opposite was true."

Abe nodded. "Great. Keep going."

"He has over twenty lots to develop with homes. He has his own framing crew but relies on subcontractors for most of his other production. And I was surprised that a lot of his business comes from word-of-mouth." Abe nodded again, encouraging me. I took a deep breath. The call with Fred seemed like a positive one, but what if I'd misread my own performance yet again? I'd thought the previous call went well, and I'd been wrong.

Regardless, I forged ahead. "Naturally the most exciting thing to me is that it's a tremendous lead. He seems genuinely interested in switching window suppliers. I made the presentation like you did, by handing him the brochure and talking about how the Acme brand will help him. I asked him if we could bid on some upcoming projects and he said blueprints would be available in two weeks. So that was a great sales call!"

Abe waited.

Oh no, I thought. *I* did *screw up.* "Or that's how I saw it," I said to him, uncertain now. "Did I come close?"

Abe smiled and turned to me. "Very good! You should know, though, that Fred might not be as interested as Hank in the ways that our brand enhances his homes. I used that presentation with Hank, but Fred is different. Hank out-markets his competition, whereas Fred prides himself on operational efficiency and cost management. Fred marches to the beat of his own drum, while Hank is the type who likes to fit in and keep up with the competition. It's subtle.

The presentation you made based on my strategy was very nicely done."

"How would you have presented differently to Fred?" I asked.

"First, I would have tried to understand his current total cost of doing business with Acorn Windows," Abe said. "If Fred is having problems, then I would like to understand what it's costing him in installation fees, service delays, and lost business. My presentation would have focused on total cost management."

"What's total cost management?"

"The price is the short-term investment in a product. The total cost is the price plus all the other factors associated with ownership. Most salespeople allow themselves to get caught up in price negotiations because they don't know how to sell the total cost of a service. When you buy a car, the price is the payment. The total cost includes the payment, maintenance, gasoline, insurance, and so forth. But for now, let's not worry too much about that."

He concluded, "Your presentation was fine for a first meeting. The most important skill to work on now is *understanding*. You did a marvelous job. Your sales skills are improving already!"

Abe paused and looked thoughtful. "You know, I'm a little concerned, though, by how easy that call was. Do you recall how long Fred said he had been buying Acorn brand windows?"

"Well, yes. He said many years."

"Exactly," Abe said with a squint. "I wonder what that means."

Abe wasn't baiting me, just contemplating the implications. "What do you think?" he asked, with genuine interest.

"It could mean he's loyal to his suppliers, which is a good thing."

"Yep, it could," Abe conceded. "He claimed to be ready to switch suppliers, agreed?"

"Yes. That's what makes it such an exciting lead."

"Either something has gone horribly wrong with Acorn," he said, "or we're being played. It's possible Fred just wanted a quote out of us to take back to Acorn. Does Fred strike you as the kind of guy who likes change?"

"He seems eager to get us involved in his upcoming project. I think he's interested in doing business." I wanted to interpret Fred's interest as sincere. I wanted to prove I was becoming a solid student, that our plan for the next step in the process was a good sign. But Abe's wisdom and experience allowed him to see farther than I could with my youthful enthusiasm.

"Fair point," he said. "Here are my thoughts. I agree with you fully on your assessment of the sales call. Very nicely done! That said, I don't agree with the value of this lead. You didn't really answer my question. Does Fred strike you as the kind of guy who likes change?"

"No," I admitted.

"Why?"

"I don't think he's renovated his office since he opened it, and it seems like Joyce has worked for him since day one," I said. "He said he'd been using the same sales agent for two decades, while noting his loyalty to Acorn extended back many years. And did you see that polyester suit he was wearing? That thing would melt before it burned." I sighed. Everything about Fred indicated he was conservative in all ways.

"It would melt before it burned! You're too much, Adam," Abe said, laughing and shaking his head. "You're right! It sure was the office of a very conservative guy. People like Fred always fascinate me. Ever hear the term 'first nickel'?"

"I think so. It's someone who's cheap, right?"

Abe laughed. "I prefer the term *frugal*, but yes. That's what it means. A guy like Fred is someone that people never expect to be rich. They say he still has his 'first nickel' and think he is cheap but fail to recognize his business acumen. People like him live conservatively and don't care what other people think. They aren't out to impress. I think Fred is the guy you never expect to be rich but is probably worth millions." Abe shrugged. "Anyway, the important thing is that you handled the sales call well, made a fine analysis, and scheduled the next step. Where are we headed now?"

We made two more sales calls that afternoon and concluded that both prospects were not solid leads. As we drove, Abe asked what I thought of the day. I told him I was excited by his lessons.

"That's nice to hear," he said. "How did you feel about the opportunities we uncovered? Which leads are hot? Which are not?"

The conversation with Abe was vastly different than the ones with Joe. Abe treated me as an adult and talked to me like a coach who was genuinely interested in helping, while Joe talked to me and other salespeople as if we were all children and he was the adult with the answers. I felt free to express my opinions with Abe as if we were talking as equals, peer to peer.

"Obviously, the superintendent who uses aluminum windows is not a good opportunity. I think the lead with Fred Deardon is the hottest lead we have. Hank Piquell said he's not ready to leave Spartan yet. But I think we have to go along with him and give him the price quote to keep building the relationship."

"I agree with you about the corn farmer," Abe said. "I'm not sure about Piquell or Deardon. It's always hard to judge those things. Sometimes you'll feel certain about a sale that never happens; other times you make a sale out of the blue that was completely unexpected. I like the Piquell lead better, but they both require equally energetic follow-up for now. You forgot to mention the first call of the day with Tom Santa at Evergreen. You never know. That could eventually turn into something, even if it takes a year or two."

We arrived at the hotel, and he invited me in for a review.

"A review already?" I asked, trying not to sound defensive. Most companies conducted reviews once or twice a year. I was about to receive one in my first week!

"Most definitely! It's probably not what you think, though. I'm not giving you a grade that will go on your permanent record," Abe said with a laugh. "I want to share my observations and how you can grow from today. Can you imagine seeing someone underperform for months and not telling them?"

"That makes a lot of sense, I guess," I said reluctantly.

"There's no point in waiting on an arbitrary schedule to provide feedback to a worker. You wouldn't let a baseball player continue swinging with a noticeable flaw. So why allow a sales performer do his job without giving regular feedback, right?"

I nodded, but my heart was sinking. Abe had been kind—up until now. I had no idea what was in store for me. I prepared myself for the worst.

10

Falling off the Tracks

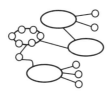

On the drive home, fatigue replaced adrenaline. I easily could have fallen asleep in the Chicago rush hour stop-and-go traffic. I had to concentrate hard on my driving and exercise the last vestiges of my mental energy to get home safely.

Abe's review had been far more intense than I'd expected, and it had left my depleted brain reeling. It was dusk by the time I arrived home, and the walk up to my second-floor apartment sapped my remaining energy. The aroma of dinner filled the hallway.

As much as I enjoyed cooking, I felt content to turn this one over to Mary. When I opened the door, she greeted me with a glowing smile and a loving kiss. "What happened? You look so tired!"

"Nothing happened. It was just a very intense day. How was your day?"

"Wonderful," she said. "The kids at school are cuter than ever. But I want to talk about *your* first day at school."

I smiled. "Do I smell pork chops in tomato sauce?" My favorite!

"Yes, you do," she said, leading me by the hand to the small table in our undersized kitchen. "I'm worried. You look really tired and you're home late. What happened? How was it?"

"It was great! Unbelievable. I learned a ton and my review went really well."

She was startled. "You got a review on your first day in the field?"

"Yes." I stopped, seeing her concern. "It wasn't bad. Just...exhausting. Abe said I did a great job. He was really pleased with my prospecting efforts. He told me I should work on my listening skills and gave me a few examples of times I interrupted during meetings. It was hard to hear some of it, but he had a way of making it all sound paternal."

I shook my head. "Mary, it was amazing to watch him in action. I think I'm going to learn so much working with him. He makes selling look so effortless— he's so calm, but very intense and focused on the other people he talks to at the same time. They open up, and every meeting seems to bring opportunities. Even people we don't want to talk to are interested after Abe finishes."

She took my hand. "That's great! Tell me everything."

"Okay, but I'm starved. Can we eat? I'm exhausted and I have to do it all over again tomorrow."

Mary served her specialty with a side of orzo and poured me a cola on ice. I took my first bites rapidly. The stewed tomatoes, garlic, and oregano wonderfully flavored the pork chop. While we ate, she asked me to tell her about some of the things I'd learned that day.

I was still dressed in my business clothes. Mary was wearing the same skirt and blouse she wore to school. "This is fun," I said. "We're like Ozzie and Harriet. Nice meal, dear. Can you grab my pipe and the newspaper?"

"Don't get too attached to that image," she replied. "And stop with the suspense. Traveling with Joe was torture, but you love traveling with Abe. What's the difference? Tell me."

I grabbed a piece of paper and drew the Non-Linear Sales Formula. I explained, "When I worked at Spartan, we were taught a linear sales method, the same one taught in books for the last hundred years. But it isn't reality. Abe has this whole new outlook on the process."

"It starts with the work you do before game day," I explained.

"Game day?" Mary asked.

"Yes. Game day," I said. "It's the day in the field when you have to make the most of your opportunities. I know that it sounds corny, but I believe it."

"Then why the glum look on your face?" Mary asked.

"Oh, that's probably just because I'm exhausted. I need to get into mental shape if I'm going to be any good at this."

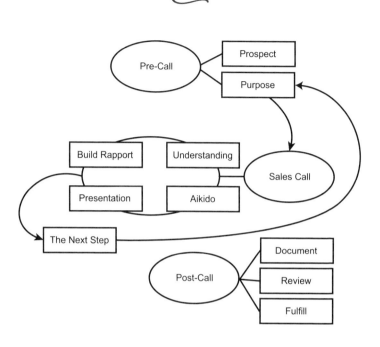

Mary took my hand. "I'm so proud of you," she said. "I've never seen you this excited about work. Tell me more about game day."

"It actually starts before game day. In Saginaw we worked the phones to set everything up for today. And, today, Abe taught me how to really run a sales meeting. It was amazing to watch. When Abe is talking to a client, he isn't trying at all to control the flow of the meeting or the client's opinions. He calls it Aikido."

"The martial art?" Mary asked.

"You've heard of it?"

"I have, but I can't see how that would help you in selling."

"I didn't either, until I watched Abe. The first prospect was hostile and Abe just let him vent until he ran out of steam. Another sales call went in perfect linear order. Some sales calls ebbed and flowed, but every time we left a sales call, Abe managed to keep the relationship growing with a prospect."

"What does Aikido have to do with it?" she asked.

"Aikido is about avoiding conflict. Rather than pressuring clients and prospects, Abe says that you should let them drive the flow of conversation. He never argued with the hostile prospect and, amazingly, the guy calmed down. We had a goal before every meeting and accomplished it every time."

Mary stopped looking at my diagram and stared into my eyes as if I were a changed man. She had always expressed her confidence in my abilities, but I think my passion and explanation of high-level sales theory surprised her.

"I think I learned more in one day than I have in my entire career," I said, not waiting for Mary to comment. "It isn't just people and process, though. Abe is emphatic about paperwork."

"Not your strong suit," she said. "You hate reports."

"Yes. But this isn't about reporting to him. It's about taking care of every sales opportunity. Abe calls them 'gems' and says that each one must be treated as a special case because you never know which ones will become your best customers. Mary, this guy has so much to teach me. It's like I'm growing just by breathing the same air he does. It's really humbling to be around someone who's so wise."

She gave me one of her million-watt smiles. We ate our meal and I asked her to tell me about her third-graders. A day never passed without a new story about funny things her kids said. "Today," she said, "I asked Scott Philips how he spells *playground*. He wrote on the board, 'p-l-a-g-r-o-w-n-d.' I told him it was incorrect. He looked at me with big eyes and said, 'But that's how *I* spell it, Mrs. Brody!'"

Eight hours of sleep later, I woke refreshed, feeling like a Jedi master. Sure, I had made my share of mistakes on my first day in the field with Abe, but my sales teacher had given me loads of great information.

The second day of sales calls with Abe went well, even though we didn't encounter the same quality of leads. After we finished the last sales call of the day—a visit to another solid lead that I'd share with one of my dealers—I dropped Abe at the airport and drove home, feeling extremely confident about my future. If I applied his knowledge, how could I go wrong?

I was excited to be on my own for a while after my first couple days with Abe. In fact, the next few weeks went by without the anxiety I'd felt that first day under Abe's scrutiny. We spoke regularly, usually on Mondays, when Abe asked me to submit a weekly game plan. I started calling on customers and began prospecting for new dealers. The work I started with builders during those first two days with Abe enhanced my credibility with dealers. They loved the sales leads I brought them. I had elevated my performance and reputation to a new level.

One night, I came home from work especially pleased with myself and cooked Mary a fantastic dinner of steak and baked potatoes. "You're looking like the cat who ate the canary," she remarked, eyeing me over the dinner table as I poured her a glass of wine.

"I've just never felt so confident in my abilities," I told her. "Abe must believe I'm doing great—he's turned me loose, and I'm achieving so much. I'm ready to take the reins entirely!"

"Uh-huh," Mary said, but she seemed suddenly distant.

"What's got into you?" I asked.

She paused. "It's just that you seem a little cocky," she confessed. "This isn't like you. You were so humble the first time you worked with Abe, telling me how much you still had to learn from him. Now you're telling me you're practically ready to replace him."

"I was hoping you'd be supportive!" I replied, stung by Mary's comment.

"Adam, I *am* supportive. You know that. I've been behind you every step of the way. But this kind of—well, bluster—isn't like you. I've never known you to be arrogant before. It's like you're taking your success for granted all of a sudden." She saw the look on my face. "I'm sorry," she said. "I shouldn't have said anything."

"No," I said curtly, pushing my chair back from the table. "It's fine. Go correct your papers. I'll clean up."

"Adam—"

"Really," I said. "It's fine."

She sighed but didn't say anything else. I washed the dishes in fuming silence.

A week or so after my argument with Mary, Abe told me he would be traveling with me again. "You know the routine," he said. "Prep two great days for us. I want to see more builders in addition to one or two stops at dealers. Our primary focus will be builders, though. Let's shoot for a two-to-one ratio at least. Got it?"

"Got it."

"Excellent."

The following Tuesday morning, I picked Abe up at his hotel. After the previous few weeks of enjoying my new sales skills, I suddenly found myself feeling more anxious than excited. As I drove the final mile towards my destination, I felt downright queasy about the day. The highlight of our two days would be a sales call to Benton Distribution. Abe had finally granted me permission to pursue them as a dealer but was insistent that I continue pursuing new builder leads for our dealers.

But I hadn't had much luck making appointments with the builders I wanted to meet. Either I couldn't get hold of anyone at the company, or the receptionist had been evasive. This meant that the sales calls I scheduled to builders for Abe's second visit were cold calls. I thought back to my argument with Mary as Abe and I entered the last stretch of road before our first stop, my stomach in knots. *Darn it,* I thought. *Why does she always have to be right?* I was about to face the fact that I had taken a step backwards, becoming the type of salesperson that Abe called a *professional visitor*—someone who pops into the offices of existing customers without appointments.

The professional visitor satisfactorily fills out call reports but fails to create credibility with clients because the salesperson's presence is a nuisance rather than a planned meeting. Joe used to compliment my call reports, failing to recognize my creative writing abilities.

For example, I once made a cold call to an office and met only a junior-level manager who, before quickly dismissing me, invited me to leave information for his boss. He suggested I call back in a couple of weeks to see if his boss was interested, leaving me wondering if he would even read the literature. It was hardly a credible lead, but on my call report I nevertheless wrote, "Met with purchasing manager who expressed strong interest in our new product. Follow-up call scheduled for two weeks." Abe would not be so easily fooled. Between Abe and Mary, I wasn't going to get away with anything at all.

Our first stop was a builder's office in Schaumburg, a suburban city on the rise. Developers were in the process of constructing a large shopping mall, and tract housing projects were popping up everywhere. I exited Route 53 at Higgins Road to visit a few of those housing developments, the first of which was being built by Gold Seal.

"You're in the lead," Abe said as we exited the car and walked onto the dry, dusty job site.

A carpentry crew pounded nails and looked none too happy to be working outside on the very chilly day. I introduced myself and received a tepid response. "Who should we talk to if we want to introduce our window products to Gold Seal?"

Two of the workers continued pounding nails, ignoring me completely. Two others paused, staring blankly at Abe and me before exchanging glances. Without taking his hand off the two-by-four he was about to nail, the man who seemed to be in charge said, "You might want to try Jan Thompson at the home office."

I thanked them for their time. Abe's silence was conspicuous, but he kept smiling as the man spoke. We'd barely gotten back in the car before he asked, "How would you rate that sales call?"

I was taken by surprise. Of course he was going to ask that, but I was out of practice. I hadn't bothered to ask it of myself once in the weeks I'd worked without his direct supervision. "It was okay," I concluded. "I give it a *B*. We got as much as we could from that stop."

"What did you get?"

"We got a contact name," I said. *That's justifies the trip, right?* But Abe wasn't going to let me off that easily.

"Jan?"

"Yes, Jan Thompson."

"Good. Is Jan a man or woman?"

"I don't know," I admitted.

"What is his or her position with the company?" Abe persisted.

"I guess I don't know that either."

"Do you suppose you might have gained that information with a phone call?" Abe asked.

I flushed. "You've made your point."

He graciously overlooked my discomfort, changing the subject. "Where's our next scheduled appointment?"

I'd arranged a meeting with an existing Acme dealer, Classic Window Design, for later in the morning. Classic Window Design was in Deerfield, ten miles north. I'd planned only cold calls prior to that meeting, including one to a custom home builder in Hinsdale—which would take us thirty minutes in the opposite direction.

"I was hoping to canvass this area for leads," I told him. The words sounded lame even before they left my mouth. Abe nodded politely and said nothing. Gone was the twinkling-eyed, fatherly teacher. This Abe was serious—and it didn't take a psychic to realize he wasn't terribly impressed with my plan.

I drove to another subdivision. Subcontractors' trucks were parked on the curbs of sites in various stages of construction. Fifteen or so homes were under roofs, and a half dozen had windows. Concrete was being poured at two locations and tradespeople were present at many of the jobsites.

The cold wind encouraged the tradesmen to work diligently just to stay warm. At each site, my presence served as an unwelcome interruption to their labor. At the last site we visited, I asked the job superintendent how I could get an introduction to the key decision-maker. He stopped in the middle of inspecting a joist and stared at me, irritable. "What?" he asked. "Who are you? Go see Ronnie at the home office."

"Ronnie who?"

"Same last name as the company: Torrentino Builders. Ronnie Torrentino," he said and turned his back on me. I stood awkwardly for a second as Abe watched.

"Uh, thanks," I said. He didn't bother to reply. Abe didn't have to say a word. *I could have gotten that information with a two-minute phone call.*

As hard as it may be to believe, the day took a turn for the *worse* as soon as we left the job site.

We drove I-294 south towards Hinsdale and hit heavy traffic. There was no way we'd make it back to Deerfield in time for our eleven o'clock meeting. Against my better judgment, I navigated aggressively through bumper-to-bumper traffic, hoping to shave precious seconds off the journey.

We arrived in Hinsdale just past ten o'clock, leaving me with an unsolvable dilemma. If this call was successful, it would make us late for our scheduled appointment with our biggest Chicago customer. If I blew the call, I'd just provide reinforcing evidence of my poor planning. There was no way I could win. Abe's silence filled the car as my heart pounded. My career suddenly felt like a train derailing in slow motion.

My temper flared. *You idiot,* I thought. *Mary was right. You got cocky, and now you're showing Abe you don't have what it takes to succeed. How could I have let this happen? How could I have planned so badly?* I was so frustrated that I nearly shouted aloud—I would've, except that would no doubt have been the last straw for Abe. Without Abe's supervision during the past few weeks, I'd become a professional visitor, mistaking activity with productivity. It is a life many salespeople lead without penalty because nobody inspects their performance, and I had fallen into the same trap.

And then, while driving, I got lost. I drove north and then backtracked south on Route 83, unable to find Hudson Custom Homes. I noticed addresses on the east side of the street had different number patterns than the west. Abe, sensing my confusion, said gently, "The west side of the street is Clarendon Hills, and the east is Hinsdale."

I drove for another minute and then lost it. I pounded the steering wheel violently. "Dammit!"

It was a vulgar display in front of a man I respected. My temper tantrum was more embarrassing than the poor sales performance. Abe was silent again. I pulled over, taking out my phone so I could call and ask for directions.

"Why sure, you can drop off some information!" the receptionist, Peggy, said pleasantly. "You know Tom Hudson's on vacation for the rest of the month, right? You'll have to come back later if you want to speak with him, I'm afraid." My heart sank. It was twenty minutes past ten and I had to make a beeline for Classic Window Design, our largest dealer in the Chicago metropolitan area. My mind raced. I decided to forego a literature drop at Hudson and instead called Classic to let them know we would be late.

Abe's silence was a mirror that revealed everything. He was surely disappointed in my performance. Even if he wasn't, I was.

After I hung up the phone, Abe recapped the morning. "We drove out of our way to interrupt the day of two workers who probably had very little to do with the selection of products they install. The information we gathered could have been gained from a phone call, which I am suspecting you didn't make to this prospect. Have I described the first sales call properly?"

I nodded, speechless and embarrassed.

"And then we drove all the way to Hinsdale, only to turn around and spend the rest of the morning in traffic. Am I right?"

I put my head in my hands as my answer.

Much to my surprise, Abe started to laugh. "I've been where you are. How does it feel?"

I was, in all honesty, on the verge of tears. Or of putting my fist through the windshield. I said, "It feels awful, Abe.

I'm so sorry. I'm embarrassed, and I feel like I've let you down."

"Nonsense!" he said. "We agree that you made a huge mistake. You failed to plan for game day. You took your past success for granted. You thought it was easy after our first two days. Yes?"

"Yes," I admitted.

"Winners don't take their performance for granted, Adam."

I stared at him. "Have you been talking to my wife?" He regarded me quizzically. "It's just that she said essentially the same thing to me a week ago," I added.

Abe chuckled. "Your wife is a very wise woman, Adam. She knows as well as I do the perils of resting on your laurels. Winners bring their A-game every day. You got comfortable these past few weeks. You gave some dealers leads they could use, and they praised you for it. You performed better than you ever had in your previous years of selling. Yes?"

If I said yes, I had performed better, it would seem hypocritical. I *was* improving as a salesperson, but saying so would only make me like one of those old-timers who failed to face the truth of their own shortcomings. "Well, yes. I learned some great things from you on the first two days. I guess I didn't prepare as well this time."

"Excellent!" he said with sincere happiness. "Now you know. You cannot hide from yourself. You showed me how your performance has deteriorated since our first coaching session. I intentionally let you work alone for a few weeks to help you discover your path. If you allow yourself to operate wastefully in anonymity, you only fool yourself.

"You have to be willing to perform under the scrutiny of an objective observer. In the absence of a coach or mentor, the objective observer must be the man in the mirror." He looked directly at me. "Do you understand?"

"Yes," I said. "I have to be objective and honest with myself about my performance."

"Very good," he said. "Hopefully you've learned something. You proved on our first days of work that you're *capable*. Now you must decide if you are *committed*. Most salespeople strive to make their best days occur when the boss is watching. Sales leaders strive to make *every* day their best day."

Abe had just forced me to stare in the mirror at a mediocre sales performer. I wanted to show him I could judge my own performance as well as he could. "I don't even want to tell you that I'm going to make it all better next time you visit," I said. "I realize I have to prove it. I have to get better. I have proven to myself that I am a very mediocre sales performer right now."

As we inched forward, Abe admonished me. "You are *not* a mediocre sales performer," he insisted. "Remember what I said before. You are a powerful perform*er* with all the talent in the world. Your perform*ance*...? Your performance today has not been good."

"That's an understatement," I agreed ruefully.

"Do you want to know what would really worry me?" Abe asked.

I was still angry with myself, but at least not feeling in jeopardy of losing my job. In fact, I felt I was closer to *career security* than ever before. I knew what to do. I knew how to do it. Abe's wise words, as always, had gotten me back on track. The only thing left for me to do was commit to a daily routine of calendar management. That was the job. In fact, I was beginning to think that maybe it was the "secret." Fill your calendar with good meetings and the rest would take care of itself.

"What would really worry you?" I asked, returning to Abe's question.

"If you didn't care, then I'd worry. Your anger is good. Your passion is powerful. I know you care. It will all get better from here."

11

The Next Step

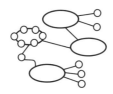

We arrived at Classic Window Design on time. Abe asked what objective I had for the meeting and was thrilled with my answer. I'd gotten a lead from a builder, Tim Thomas, who I'd met in the posh suburb of Lake Forest. Tim had asked for a list of Acme dealers, but instead of providing a list, I told him it would be better for me to deliver his information to the specific salesperson I thought was best suited to his needs. In this case, that dealer was Classic. Abe gushed with compliments.

Abe appreciated that I took control of the lead. Giving out names of dealers would only serve to frustrate the dealers by starting a bidding war, so it seemed natural for me to find the right salesperson for the builder. "Besides," I said, "if I give out random names, dealers won't recognize the value of my efforts. They won't know I generated the lead."

"Excellent," Abe said. "That's exactly how you should handle the situation."

The day was improving rapidly. I gave the builder's information to Paul Lafontaine, the top salesperson at Classic. He expressed appreciation and promised to contact the builder within the next two days. I offered to introduce him to the builder, but he said he would go alone.

We also met with Bob Renquist, Classic's owner, who Abe had known for ten years. Bob was a longtime Acme dealer with a solid business operation. His company occupied a storefront on a commercial stretch of a four-lane highway. Fast food restaurants and retail stores lined the street, and Bob's signage provided an ample marketing presence.

Bob was a conservative businessman who avoided risk. He was thoughtful, quiet, and patient. I discovered instantly that, rather than engage in idle chitchat, he would not welcome a rambling conversation about golf or personal hobbies. I purposefully kept dialogue focused on business issues. His thinning blonde hair and blue eyes complemented his Scandinavian complexion. He stood a full head taller than Abe and I. He shook my hand with a strength that surprised me. He was a quintessential professional who created an inviting calm throughout his organization, which probably contributed to its success.

I told Bob about the lead we shared with Paul, including details about the builder. He thanked me and asked when I would be going with Paul on a visit.

"I offered. Paul said he'd go on his own," I said.

"I'll talk to him," Bob said. "You brought the lead and know the builder. I think you should be involved, at least to introduce Paul."

"That would be great, Bob," Abe interjected.

"What else can I do for you gentlemen?" Bob asked.

Suddenly, I was lost. Now I understood why Abe said you needed a purpose. Without one, you risk turning the business meeting into a social visit. "We're okay," I said. "Is there anything we can do for you today?"

Bob laughed. "Normally I'd tell you to go bring me some business, but it seems you already have!"

I was proud to hear that, and grateful that he made the comment in front of Abe. "Well, I'll try to do that some more. Other than that, is there anything we can do for you?"

I should have known exactly what Bob would say in response to my question. Abe had taught me not to ask, "What else can I do for you?" He assured me the answer is always the same, and he was right! People always say something dismissive like, "We're all set," or, "We're good for now."

"It's like when a retail clerk asks, 'Can I help you?' You always say, 'No thanks, I'm just looking,'" Abe had explained.

"What questions would you ask if you were a retail clerk?" I had wanted to know from Abe.

"There are so many! 'What's changing in your life that brought you into our store tonight?' or 'Welcome—please tell me what you're looking for, and I'll point you in the right direction.' Or even, 'Let me guess—you're just looking!' Those aren't perfect questions, but they're better than 'May I help you?'!"

I had been amazed at Abe's response. "You didn't seem to think for a second about those great questions," I said.

"Don't be silly. I've thought at great length about those questions, which is exactly the point. If you don't think about them beforehand, you will always lose in the heat of battle. Asking a business client 'What else can I do for you?' is like asking them to tell you how to do your job. A great sales leader takes customers in the direction they need to go."

Now, in Bob Renquist's office, Abe's theory was validated. "I think we're all set," Bob said politely in response to my tepid question. I had no other direction in which to take the meeting.

I cleared my throat, and Bob looked at me expectantly.

"Adam," Abe prompted smoothly. "Have you had a chance to tell Bob about the new technology that's been evolving in energy testing?"

I practically slapped my forehead. *Geez, Adam! Way to go!* I wished I'd thought of the subject before Abe. It was an important evolution in the industry, and Bob would be the type of person interested in the development.

"Have you heard of the new energy testing standards being promoted for windows?" I asked Bob.

"It's been written up in *Glass* magazine," he said. "I'm not sure I understand it, and I'm a little doubtful that people are going to care all that much about energy ratings on products. But, what is Acme doing about it?" He asked Abe, but Abe looked at me. *He's letting me take the lead,* I thought, and I was pleased Abe seemed to trust me on this one despite my epic failure of the morning.

"Well, we're testing all of our products now. Many building products will soon be required to meet energy standards. In the case of windows, this includes air infiltration, solar heat gain, and more. For now the standards are voluntary. But if you pass their testing criteria, you can put a label on your products that validates your product's efficiency. There could be a whole new movement brewing. I hear people calling it 'green' building. It's going to be a big thing, I think."

"Do you really think that?" Abe asked.

I was surprised by his question but held to my conviction. "Yes. I do!"

Bob asked, "Why do you believe that?"

"I see this as a big industry trend that will impact how we harvest wood, recycle materials, and regulate construction. This might only be the tip of the iceberg. Local building codes are starting to change, and I think this trend will continue to modify even national building codes. I'm not sure I like how complicated it might all become once the government gets involved. But I do believe it's a good thing that Acme is getting out in front of it."

I assured both of them that the energy technology was new and would probably get better. "Windows are the weakest part of the wall—and not just the weakest in structure. I'm talking about thermal performance properties. People want their homes to be more energy-efficient, and this testing will ensure it."

Abe looked at Bob and smiled. "The kid knows his stuff."

As we passed Paul's cubicle on our way out, Bob stopped to ask about the lead for Tim Thomas Homes. Paul said he'd be calling that day. Bob suggested a different approach. "Why don't you tell Adam what days you're available next week to meet him up north? It's his lead. Let him introduce you. After that, you two can transfer the administrative details and sales role to Paul. Make sense, guys?"

Paul agreed reluctantly. I could see he was avoiding the same experience I had just endured with Abe. Paul didn't want to live his career out loud, under the scrutiny of an observer. If Paul had gone to Tim Thomas and lost the sale, he could have easily made any number of excuses for failure. But now he was being held accountable to perform under watchful eyes—in this case, mine!

At the time I took no great pride in my leadership role. I wasn't thinking about mentoring Paul or any other salesperson. I only wanted the sale, although I was grateful for Bob's acknowledgment that I'd earned a right to be involved. I was thrilled to be of value to my customer and left the meeting feeling quite proud of myself.

"How would you rate the meeting with Bob?" Abe asked in the car.

I had forgotten *again* to expect that question, even though Abe asked it every time. *You have to plan for this question,* I thought. *And you have to ask it of yourself.*

"I think it was an *A* sales call," I said. "We gave a good lead and proved to be of value to our client. I felt great about describing the new window technology. I think Bob was appreciative."

Abe smiled. "I agree. A good sales call."

Finally! I thought and allowed myself to exhale.

"So what's next?" Abe asked.

I told him sheepishly that I only had cold calls lined up for the afternoon.

"No, I mean what's next with Bob and Classic Windows?"

"Oh!" I said, catching on. "Well, I guess I'll call Paul to find out when he is available to meet Tim Thomas and follow up with Bob in the next couple of weeks."

"What's the follow-up with Bob?" Abe asked.

"I don't understand."

"What's the next step? What do you have to offer Bob?"

I hesitated. "I don't know."

"Then the call rates a *B*," Abe said. "The call has to be better to merit an *A*. Remember how I showed you to schedule the next step?"

"I usually do with prospects," I said. "It's harder with customers that I call on repeatedly."

"Nonsense," Abe said. "You did a marvelous job of explaining the new energy standards. You could have scheduled a follow-up meeting to show Bob samples of the energy labels and literature that highlights the program. You could have asked Paul what dates he had available instead of planning the extra step of phoning later. Those were the easy next-step opportunities."

Abe continued, "There were advanced levels of opportunity that veteran sales performers would have discovered. You could have suggested a meeting with the staff members to teach them about the new energy standards. You could have suggested a meeting to discuss target builders you want to pursue with Paul or other salespeople in the organization. You had a few options. Do you see?"

I nodded. I didn't feel defensive—just insecure and apologetic. "I'm not sure I'll see all the things you do, Abe."

"Are you looking?"

Wow. That was a powerful question.

"I think I am?"

Abe raised one eyebrow at me.

"No," I concluded. "I wasn't. I just wanted to have a good meeting. I wasn't thinking about the next step."

Abe patted my arm. "Good. Now you know what needs to happen. Nicely done, Adam. It was, in fact, a wonderful meeting. I enjoyed watching you in action there. You're a good salesperson and an excellent presenter. I particularly loved the conviction with which you sold the new energy standards. It was very persuasive."

"I meant to ask you, Abe. I was surprised when you doubted it would be the next big thing."

"Did I doubt it?" Abe asked.

"I thought you did."

"No. Think back. I merely asked why *you* thought highly about it."

"I guess you did. But," I asked, "*do* you think it will be a big thing?"

"Yes. Revolutionary to the industry."

"Then why did you ask me if I thought so, if *you* already thought so?"

"Welcome to team selling, son."

I laughed, amazed that the tragedy of my morning had melted away. Other supervisors would have held the morning against me for weeks, if not years. For Abe it was just a teaching moment. As long as I chose to learn from it, he'd continue to support me. Every day I worked with Abe, my respect for him grew.

"Listen, Adam," he said. "It's been a rough first day. Why don't you go home and work on making tomorrow a better one, instead of spending the afternoon cold calling." He laughed when he saw my expression. "I thought you'd be relieved, even if you *do* still have to spend the afternoon working!"

Mary was surprised to see me home so early when she got back to the apartment. I confessed that the morning had been awful.

She had no sympathy. "Then I'll let you do the work to make tomorrow better."

"It was really bad," I said.

"Tomorrow will be better."

"I don't know. I'm really struggling."

"The past is over. Forget it. You'll be fine. If it were easy, everyone would do it." Mary never had any patience with my self-pity, but I needed to do more than snap out of my funk. I owed her an apology. I took a deep breath.

"Listen," I said. "I was wrong the other night, and you were right. I *was* taking my success for granted, and that's why I failed today. I'm sorry."

She eyed me sternly, but the corner of her mouth was twitching. "I'm not accepting any apologies that don't come with an offer of dish duty. For a week."

"A week!" I protested. "I wasn't *that* pig-headed!" She gave me a look. "Okay, okay," I admitted. "I *was* that pig-headed. Deal." She cackled in triumph.

No more feeling sorry for myself. Abe was right—and so was Mary. I had to work harder. For the rest of the afternoon, that's what I did.

My diligence paid off. I made two appointments for the next day, one with a lumberyard and the other with a builder. Neither lead would turn out to hold much promise the next day. But at least I'd put some scheduled activity into the calendar. Abe's nod of approval at the end of the day made all my effort worth it. And...

I never had a bad day like that again. I wasn't just working for myself—I also couldn't let Abe and Mary down. They believed in my abilities, and I was determined not to disappoint them. After that disastrous day, I started every sales call with the idea of creating a next step at the end of the meeting. As Abe said, it was always possible to find something ... as long as you looked for it.

Abe traveled with me again a couple of months later. I had packed the calendar. We met Hank Piquell and included Jerry, a salesperson from an Acme dealer. Jerry and I were putting the final touches on the first order of what would become a long-term relationship with Crestview Builders. Abe asked about Deardon Homes. He'd been right all along—Fred wasn't interested in making a change of suppliers but had requested a proposal. I suspected he was using us to keep his existing supplier honest, just as Abe had theorized.

Abe asked me about Tim Thomas and my work with Paul. Tim had verbally committed to use our products on future homes. Paul was keeping me informed of his progress—albeit reluctantly. Much to Abe's delight, I added that Paul probably figured I would not give him more leads if he didn't keep me in the loop. "You're learning!" he said gleefully. "What about Tom Santa, that angry fellow who had the bad experience with Acme when you were in the seventh grade?"

I'd called Tom to follow up, as Abe had suggested, and he'd told me he appreciated my courage but he had no interest in our products. I let it drop. "Keep in touch," Abe suggested. "You never know."

Of course, as with most things sales-related, Abe turned out to be right. Two years later Tom would call out of the blue—much to my surprise—to ask if I'd like to get together for a discussion about a project in the works. Eventually he became a client. Like Abe had told me, the Aikido method produces results—even if they are slow to come.

Over the ensuing months, my time with Abe dwindled as he devoted energy to other salespeople and strategic planning issues. He later hired two new salespeople that he asked me to mentor as he had mentored me. My heart flooded with pride at the knowledge that Abe had faith in my ability to be a leader. I'd learned so much working for him, and I was ready to share the wisdom he'd given me. My territory began to thrive, and Abe complimented me on achieving better results than expected. Acme was a vast change from the pressure cooker I had lived in only a year earlier. For the first time in my life, I had a career.

One sunny Monday morning I called Abe and was pleased to find him in his office for once. "What gives, my man? You never write. You never call. Should I be worried?"

Abe laughed. "When you don't hear from me, it's a sure sign that you do *not* need to worry."

"We haven't traveled in a while. You should come to Chicago," I suggested.

"You're doing just fine. You don't need me there," he said.

"No," I said. "But you need me. You need to get out and have some fun selling. I know you're caught up in a lot of high-level challenges. Come travel with me and have some fun. It'll do you good to keep in practice. I'll whip you back into sales shape."

There was a long pause. I had heard through the company grapevine that Abe had been under pressure from the higher-ups, and he'd had to let go a salesperson who'd been performing abysmally. I knew if there was any truth to the rumors, Abe would be having a hard time. His generous spirit always led him to see the best in people and encourage them to succeed, and I imagined Abe would have a more difficult time than most people firing someone. Even for Abe, this job wasn't always easy.

"You know," he said finally, "that's not a bad idea. I'd love to have some time in the field with you again, Adam." I beamed. Even though I knew Abe couldn't see me, he could probably tell from my voice that I was smiling. That was one of the first lessons I'd learned from him.

"Great," I said. I wanted to tell him how much it meant to me that this time we'd be traveling as colleagues—and equals—but I realized he probably knew. I'd come a long way under his tutelage.

Two weeks later we were on the road, taking turns being in the lead on sales calls. I'd run one meeting, and Abe would run the next. I took care of filling our calendar, and we had a grand time working the territory for a couple of days. After every meeting, we'd ask each other to rate our calls—this time, the conversations felt jovial, not stressful, but Abe still took them seriously, and so did I.

After one particularly successful meeting, Abe turned to me in the car. "I can't tell you how proud of you I am, Adam," he said quietly. "I've watched you grow from an impetuous kid with raw talent to a true professional. It's a pleasure to be working with you." My heart leaped. Abe had always been effusive with his praise, but this was different. This was as if he'd handed me a trophy. Out of all the accolades I earned over the course of my career as a salesperson, those two sentences from Abe remain the highest honor.

We went to lunch at a favorite diner of mine near Wrigley Field. "You know, there's one thing you never told me," I said while we waited for our burgers.

"What's that?"

"The secret. You never told me the sales secret."

Abe sat back and chuckled. "I didn't? Do you mean to say you haven't figured it out by now?"

"How the heck could I have figured it out? You've never even given me a clue!"

"You've been living it, Adam. You just don't know it. The sales secret is the method to closing more sales."

"Do you mean Aikido?"

"Aikido is a tool, not the secret."

"I don't understand," I said. I was no longer insecure about my skills. I happily admitted my faults and recognized my mistakes were new learning opportunities. I was hungry for more knowledge.

"Do you remember, during your very first interview, when I asked how you close a sale?"

"I remember you asking me, yes. I don't remember my answer," I admitted.

"Think about it. Your answer was perfect then and you live it now. That's the sales secret."

I pondered the question out loud. "How do I close?" I looked at Abe. "I think closing is a series of little victories."

"Yes!" Abe said. "That's it. Go on."

"Well... Remember that first call we went on together with Hank Piquell, the high-end custom builder? We set up the first meeting with a phone call. That meeting went well and built momentum. We agreed to follow up and got some blueprints. The fact that we didn't initially get his business didn't stop me from calling again. I contacted Steve Victor, the builder we knew in common—he pushed Hank to give us a try in spite of our higher price, and that helped. Hank tried us once. He said our product was better, while our delivery and service offset the price by reducing his costs and the 'hassle factor.'"

"Good," Abe said. "So when did you close the sale? Was it the signature on the first order? Was it the good timing of our first phone call? Was it Steve's prodding, or was it the inefficiency of our competition? Which was it?"

I saw the answer. "All of it!"

"Precisely! The first appointment you set while working in Saginaw was a 'close'. The fact that we listened carefully to his challenges on the first meeting enabled us to earn the right for a follow-up meeting, another 'close'. The fact that you had Steve Victor contact Hank was a 'close'. You involved Jerry to price the project right and presented in a way that gave Hank confidence, another 'close'. By the time you took the order, were you worried?"

"No," I said.

"Did you feel tension or any pressure to 'ask for the order'?"

"No," I said. "I think that all the little things we did leading up to the order were part of the incremental process of success."

"Exactly," Abe said. "Closing is incremental."

"Closing is opening a new relationship. Closing is proactively seeking and listening for opportunities for the next step."

Abe paused and looked at me, "Closing is a series of little victories, just like you said. Keep building little victories and creating momentum in your business relationship and the sales will come. That, my friend Adam, is the secret."

"You know, Adam, there are two things that make winning salespeople," Abe said. "The first is an insatiable desire for growth. It includes a willingness to challenge yourself. You had it from the start. I loved the day you hit the steering wheel and swore. I knew instantly you would never let a bad day like that happen again." He added, "I'm just glad you didn't break the steering wheel."

"I think I injured the palm of my hand instead."

"It's our secret," he said with a wink.

"In addition to growth, the other success factor is calendar management," he said. "As you've learned, if you fill your calendar with productive meetings, the results will come. Proactively seek the 'next step' every time. The purpose for the sales call is the reason you ended the last one. The goal for each sales call is to create a purpose for the next one."

"So the calendar is like the Salesperson's most important weapon."

"I like to think of it as a tool," Abe said. "But yes! That's it exactly. You constantly look for ways to help. Ask yourself, 'what's in it for them?'—'them' of course being your clients. The key is genuinely wanting success for your *clients*. Sales isn't about pushing products. It's about wanting to truly help people. Then they are anxious to have you in their offices. Yes?"

"Yes," I said, seeing it clearly. "It's a cycle. I can see it working in all facets of selling."

"What does a dentist do at the conclusion of a cleaning?" he asked me.

"He schedules the next cleaning."

"Precisely. What does a hairstylist do at the conclusion of the haircut?" he asked.

"Schedules the next haircut," I said, drawing the obvious conclusion.

"No," Abe said. "Only the good ones. The others let a client walk out the door and hope to get a return visitor. The good ones do not leave their success to chance. This is another important aspect of the sales secret. Proficient sales performers consciously manage their calendar. The weak ones fail to schedule the next meeting."

"The challenge is figuring out the next step," I said. "That's the hard part."

"Yes, very good," Abe said. "The sales secret is simply bringing to the forefront of your consciousness the thing you knew subconsciously when I interviewed you a few years ago: closing is incremental. The challenge is being on alert for the next step. It's not easy to see. It takes practice and is acquired only through wisdom."

"What do you really mean by wisdom? I think I get it, but I want to be sure."

"Adam Brody, what I mean is that wisdom cannot be taught, only acquired. I can teach you science and tell you that it takes an afternoon of fifty phone calls to make two appointments. I can even quantify the information you gather about a prospect and measure the quality of your travel time in the field with ratios of windshield time to face time.

"I can measure your product knowledge and assess the size of your contact list and count how many people you know at a given client office. I can teach you instantly how to succeed in the scientific aspect of selling. But I can't teach wisdom.

"Wisdom is acquired only with time and experience. Time alone is not enough," he said emphatically. "You must pay attention. That's why you should always be looking for the 'next step' in the process. It takes time to see it."

"I think you're saying that *wisdom is knowledge applied.*"

He leaned back and said, "Yes! Perfect. That is wisdom. I can yell at my children, but they're going to make mistakes anyway. So instead of yelling, I teach them knowledge and hope they apply it to their experiences. Do you see?"

"I do. You told me all along that the next step was the sales secret. You constantly pushed me to schedule follow-up meetings by seeking the next opportunities to help my clients. But I had to look for them repeatedly before I gained the wisdom to recognize them on my own."

"You had the knowledge that I gave you," Abe said. "Then it took the many months of experience for you to become expert at applying it. You had to discover ways to help your clients by creating each 'next step' in the process. You tuned in to your clients' wants, needs, dreams, and desires. The client knows you want to make a sale. The wisdom is the ability to know how you can help the client."

"The next step was the secret all along!" I said. I remembered my belligerent determination to weasel the secret out of Abe and laughed aloud. I'd known it the whole time. It had just taken the wisdom of experience for me to see it.

Our burgers arrived. "Mmmm. I told you these were good!" I said after we'd swallowed our first bites.

Abe wiped the corner of his mouth and said, "Better than good! Delicious! There is nothing better than a good burger and a cup of coffee. Adds to your longevity."

"Yeah, well," I said. "I still don't get the hot coffee with your lunch."

"You're young," he said with a gleam. "You'll get it soon enough. Wisdom, my boy. Wisdom."

12

The Legacy

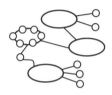

Not surprisingly, Abe eventually outgrew his role at Acme and started his own sales consulting company. He obtained several clients out West and decided to move with his wife to California, where he thrived on the year-round outdoor exercise. We spoke regularly on the phone—Abe used email, but he never learned to love it, always preferring more direct methods of communication. I asked him once if he was thinking about retiring. "If you are helping people and love what you do, why retire?" he responded. That was Abe.

In our conversations, we talked about our families, our lives, and our businesses. He treated me as a peer even though we both knew it was his leadership that had pushed me to grow as much as I had. I'd risen through the ranks at Acme, and when Abe left the company I replaced him as vice president. I accepted his former title with a great sense of pride and responsibility. It was now my task, and my privilege, to transfer Abe's lessons to other salespeople.

I have seen his theory work hundreds of times over the years. I still use Abe's methods to slowly reveal to new salespeople the secret hidden within the Non-Linear Sales Formula.

In sales, as in life, the attempt to control every situation creates tension. Acceptance of the non-linear sales reality allows us to deal with situations as they arise, think on our feet, and allow the people around us—whether loved ones or clients—to determine the proper timing for their decisions.

"Happiness," it was said, "is wanting what you have, not having what you want." This occurs in the selling profession when you focus on the process and accept that the results will naturally occur. Measurements of success are based on activities within the salesperson's control, with the faith that end results will occur...and they do.

As I have mentored my people in the ways of the sales secret, I have tried to give them the same gift that Abe once gave me: a means to achieve happiness in a profession that was once known only for its pursuit of material gain. What Abe taught me is that the art and science of sales can be meaningful, even spiritual. When you set a clear focus on finding the right solution for your customer, the process of selling becomes the joy, and material gain becomes the incidental reward. This is my own sales secret.

Abe showed me that a genuine interest in the well-being of other people made a great salesperson; not coincidentally, it also made a better person. His lessons applied to every aspect of my life.

Abe's diagram of the Non-Linear Sales Formula hangs now on my office wall.

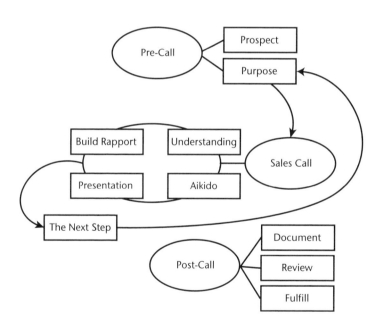

Abe promised me that wisdom would be the development of knowledge from personal experience. The process he taught gave me the intelligence to adopt a systematic method for selling. But time and experience provided the tools for personal growth. I continually learn more by trusting the process and discovering ways in which Abe's Non-Linear Sales Formula and the sales secret deliver beneficial results to my clients while making my company profitable.

One salesperson after another at Acme has discovered the truth of this formula. New salespeople are happy to learn how pressure for instant results can be replaced with a manageable process; veteran salespeople recognize, as I did many years earlier, that this is the exact method by which they have created sales success all along.

Closing is incremental.

Closing is timing.

Closing is listening.

Closing is calendar management, created by continually seeking the next step throughout the business relationship.

The Non-Linear Sales Formula replaces the *transactional* mindset of linear thinking with an empathetic *relationship* mindset. Setting appointments with purpose creates sales momentum. The relationship grows with each dialogue and culminates in the first transaction. The salesperson does not force the timing of the sale but instead discovers when the timing is right for the client.

One Friday night in mid-December, Mary and I were preparing dinner. Our lives had gotten exponentially busier as we'd gotten older, and our family now included our fourteen-year-old daughter, Madeline.

"I haven't talked to Abe in a while," I said. The thought came to me out of nowhere. The words were barely out of my mouth when my phone buzzed in my pocket. Dread flashed through me. Somehow, I knew it wasn't good news.

"Don't answer it," Mary said.

But I did. I knew what I'd hear before the caller spoke. I walked away from the table to hear the news.

After a few minutes of my listening and "mm-hmm-ing", Mary crossed the kitchen to take my hand and whispered, "Adam?"

"Dad?" Madeline asked. "Dad, are you okay?" She'd never seen her father cry. Mary took the phone out of my hand and set in on the counter.

"It's Abe, isn't it," she said.

I couldn't bring myself to speak. I just nodded.

She wrapped her arms around me and placed her head against my chest. The man who had changed my life two decades earlier was gone forever.

We flew the next day to Palm Springs, California to attend Abe's funeral. Twelve hundred people attended—an astounding gathering, especially considering that Abe had lived most of his life in the Midwest and the ceremony occurred less than forty-eight hours after his passing. Hundreds of people from the area showed up, although Abe had only lived in California for eight years. More than two hundred business associates had flown in from around the country, including people like Steve Victor and Bob Renquist.

Members of Abe's private country club, people from the local cycling community, business associates, old friends, and people who'd barely known him packed the synagogue. They all had stories to share about ways in which the man had impacted their lives. But the anecdotes from people who were near-strangers were perhaps the most moving testament to the consistency with which Abe lived his life. A nurse described how Abe had offered *her* solace as he sat in the hospital waiting room with a painfully fractured leg. Two women from the local grocery store came to honor him because he was a regular customer who brought them candies and told silly jokes. The stories kept coming.

For each person who had a story to share, like me, there were dozens more sharing theirs, too. The effects of Abe's presence on earth rippled across thousands of miles. His wisdom, love, and patience had touched the souls of people from all walks of life. Looking out over the diverse group of people gathered to celebrate his life, I realized that Abe had inspired countless people—who in turn had shaped the lives of many other people. The impact of

Abe's life was exponential. He was a leader who produced more leaders.

His son Thomas, lithe and a strikingly similar version of a young Abe, delivered the eulogy. Thomas thanked everyone for the outpouring of love displayed over the previous two days. He told us that Abe had grown up without a father and been raised by a mother struggling for economic survival. After dropping out of high school to earn money to support his family, Abe eventually earned a general education degree and later put himself through Wayne State University in Detroit while working nights as a stadium vendor for the Tigers and Red Wings. "My father made everything look easy," Thomas said, "but that's because he worked so hard to prepare." He looked down at his written script. "The measure of a man is not the riches he has accumulated," he muttered. "It is not the success he measures in business. The success of a man..."

He paused, nearly breaking down. To my surprise, he crumpled the paper he was reading from and looked directly at us, abandoning the contrived and formal words he'd written down and speaking from his heart. "The thing that I learned most from my father, Abraham Isaacson, is that your willingness to give unselfishly is the measure of love in your heart. My father taught me to love freely and recognize that every person has a unique story. He once told me that every person is both a hero and a wounded soul in the same package. He told me it is up to us to help others find the courage in their hearts to overcome the baggage they carry and help them emerge as heroes to others."

After the funeral, Mary and I paid our respects at the Isaacson home. I watched as Abe's wife, Rose, eased the pain of the wounded souls that came to her chair. Like Abe, she had so much to give other people in need, even in the midst of her own pain. At last, it was my turn to sit with her.

"I'm so sorry, Rose," I said. "I don't even know what to say. There aren't words enough to express the loss I feel."

"Adam," she said, holding my right hand in one frail hand while patting me gently with her other. "Abe simply adored you and always knew you'd be successful. You were a shining light for him in a difficult time. Did you know that the year he hired you, his best friend had been killed in a motorcycle accident? It was a tough time, and then you came along. You were his favorite student. I bet you didn't know that."

With tears in my eyes, I confessed that it was news to me. "I had no idea. He was so amazingly positive when he trained me, and he never once flagged in his efforts to support me. In spite of any grief he must have been feeling, he always stayed upbeat and kept a focus on helping me grow." Rose smiled at me as we both struggled to hold back tears. "I felt we had a powerful connection. He was fatherly to me. He pushed me, but he always cared."

She said definitively. "You were the 'one' to him. He wanted someone to carry on his legacy. He had a lot of unique ideas to share and was eager to find someone to listen. You meant a lot to him. He felt lucky to find you."

"I only hope he knew how much he has meant to my life."

"He knows, dear. He knows," she said, smiling through her tears.

On my return flight, the plane carried us over the Rocky Mountains on a cloudless afternoon. Looking down at the majestic landscape, I recalled the lessons of my mentor and recognized he was now blending in with the earth below. Dust to dust...

Mary squeezed my hand knowingly. "Thank you," she said. "I'm glad you brought me. I'm glad you trusted him and let him teach you and that you introduced me to him. It was an honor. He's in you, honey. Now you are carrying his torch."

"He lives in a lot of people," I said.

I looked out the window, and the memory of my first days as a salesperson drifted into my mind. I'd been so ashamed of myself at the career path I'd fallen into—and now look at me. Thanks to Abe I'd come to realize that selling is like any other career; you can choose to do it badly, or you can choose to do it well. Any path can lead to growth and joy.

In truth, a salesperson can be a wonderful source of help. There is honor in becoming the salesperson who helps people achieve their goals in life. People need clothing, cars, houses, and utensils with which they can cook. They want the pleasure of an outdoor grill, fabrics to decorate their homes, and gifts to share with loved ones. They require the use of a computer, desk, and copier in order to make a living. They have to buy these things from someone and only hope to find a trustworthy representative.

Abe taught me that sales leaders help people acquire material goods but also reminded me that salespeople bear the weight of an organization on their shoulders. Not only are salespeople held accountable for the success of their clients, but they also bear the responsibility for the profitability of their own co-workers. They are the frontline warriors fighting for the success of their companies.

I learned from Abe that success requires tremendous discipline. He showed me that it took hard work to make the job easy. He demonstrated how to apply pressure to myself and develop the necessary skills that effortlessly close sales. "Success is easy when you work very hard," Abe used to say.

As I looked down at the rocky landscape, I recalled how Abe frequently deflected tension with humor. His persuasion came from a loving heart, not aggression. His success came from easy gestures and calm actions. He believed all business associates—clients and co-workers alike—had the right to their opinions.

Abe helped me master the art of non-conflict in Aikido selling. Abe proved that presentations could be concise and effective. He demonstrated how to understand clients without interrogating them. "The results," he frequently said, "will take care of themselves, if you do the right things."

Abe's secret can live on in me, I thought. Some people say that life is a journey, not a destination, but Abe's wisdom tells me otherwise.

The destiny of a soul is measured by the accomplishments of the human spirit. In that sense, life is a both a journey and a destination: it's a journey with purpose. This truth exists in the pursuit of short-term goals, even when twists and turns take one off course, as well as the pursuit of long-term life achievements. A life without a purpose, without a destination, leads nowhere.

I try to remind myself regularly that being a salesperson is a privilege. I recognize that my career has afforded me the opportunity to impact many lives. I remembered the words Abe shared with me the first time we traveled. He proved that success is measured not only in the dollars and cents of business, but also in the contributions made to the success and happiness of others.

"Reduce your expectations of personal gain and increase your desire to help other people," he said. "It is the only way you will ever acquire anything in life."

I held Mary's hand as I looked out over the marvelous landscape while basking in gratefulness.

I thought about that day on campus when I met Mary and launched a partnership with the most amazing woman I've ever known. I reminisced about the first interview that I had with Abe Isaacson and about how fortunate I was to continue his legacy by sharing his knowledge with others.

Like anyone, I have ups and downs and continue to struggle at times. But mostly I feel fortunate to lead a life that enables me to learn and grow every day. I've discovered that I work in a profession with meaning. I can offer contributions to the lives of others that ultimately change the world in very positive ways.

My name is Adam. I am a salesman.

Group Discussion Questions

Chapter 1

- Does Joe's goal-setting process resemble actual practices in any way? What could be done to improve it? What are the biggest problems with his goal-setting process?
- Is Adam's description of "bobble head" listening mode accurate? If so, what should a salesperson do to deal with this bad habit?
- Discuss the "vapid platitudes" that Adam describes. Is "no" the beginning of the sale? Is it necessary to be "friends" with your customers? Does it really work to get prospects robotically saying "yes" with the belief that they will eventually become more agreeable to buying from you? Are open-ended questions the only "right" questions?
- What are the implications of Joe's behavior during his joint sales calls with Adam? Was he coaching or showing off? What can you learn about conducting a joint sales call more effectively from the errors that Joe made?

Chapter 2

- Discuss Martin Seligman's concept of gratification versus pleasure. Is it appropriate to the sales profession?
- Discuss the assertion that results and material gain are not necessarily proof of sales competence. Which salespeople have you met who get results in spite of poor performance?
- Does the constant need to get "more" sales and achieve higher quotas create anxiety? If so, is the pursuit of performance excellence (rather than solely focusing on results) a viable coping mechanism? Why or why not?
- What were some of the raw materials that Adam possessed that made him a solid candidate for success?
- Rabbi Schactel's comment is, "Happiness is wanting what you have, not having what you want." What is the significance of his statement? Is there a place for this philosophy in selling?

Chapter 3

- What is the purpose of Abe sharing Lao Tzu's wisdom, "It's better to know and think you don't, than to not know and think you do." What does this statement imply about any person in his or her career?

- Adam asserts that any expert begins by failing. How does this apply to your own experiences? How important is it to be honest with yourself about your own failures? What failures in your professional experience have taught you the most?
- What are your thoughts on the Linear Sales Diagram that Adam shares during his first interview? Discuss in what ways you believe this concept is realistic or, conversely, only theoretical.
- How is "follow up" different than Abe's concept of "fulfillment"? How should the concept of fulfillment affect sales behaviors throughout the business relationship?
- Abe is pleased to discover that Adam is intent on gaining personal growth and career security. How important are these characteristics to individual success? Discuss the difference between job security and career security.

Chapter 4

- Why did Adam sense he was getting the job during the second interview? What does this imply about Adam's selling skills? Hint: Describe how he listened for "buying signals."
- Throughout the book, the recurring theme is the evolution of Adam as a maturing salesperson. What are the aspects of his story that indicate he is evolving? Are these the types of growth

experiences all salespeople should seek? Why or why not?

- Abe indicated that Adam has the secret already. What is he referring to? Adam doesn't even realize it himself; so how does this relate to the wisdom of Lao Tzu?

Chapter 5

- Explore whether or not a veteran salesperson should be held to the same level of prospecting accountability as a rookie. Discuss Adam's statement that many salespeople go through entire careers without developing their prospecting skills. Is it valid? How could a salesperson avoid prospecting and still get results?

- Discuss the idea of making hundreds of prospecting calls to launch a sales campaign. Is this realistic? If a salesperson cannot prospect and produce sales from "scratch," what does this say about his or her skills?

- Why would Abe begin Adam's apprenticeship by giving minimal instructions?

- Why is Abe's presentation of the calendar so dramatic? Is it as important as he implies? Why or why not?

- Discuss Abe's belief that the only thing you can sell is a service. Even if you are promoting a product, how are you really selling only a "service?"

- How real were Adam's phone calls and the rejection he experienced? Describe your experiences with cold-calling. How does a salesperson get better at it?
- What was the difference between Abe's prospecting efforts and Adam's?
- What do you think about the idea of "understanding the prospect" as a legitimate reason for an initial dialogue?
- Why is *prospecting* so essential to achieving career security?

Chapter 6

- What does it mean when Abe says that you will be "compared to salespeople that you can't see?"
- Discuss the Non-Linear aspect of the sales call as Abe envisions it. Is it realistic? How can accepting Abe's imagery help a salesperson cope with the challenges of the sales process?
- Discuss the irony of Abe using the Socratic method to illustrate the power of Aikido selling.
- Discuss how Abe used Aikido in the first meeting with the hostile client.
- What benefits exist when you do not presume a client should do business with you?

Chapter 7

- Discuss the sales call with Hank Piquell. What worked? What would you have done differently?

What was realistic about the description of this call? Define how the sales call illustrated the relative skill levels of Adam and Abe.

- How do you think Joe would have handled the sales call with Hank Piquell?

- Abe was told by Hank Piquell on the phone that he was satisfied with his current supplier. Hank revealed a different story in the appointment. How does this demonstrate the importance of listening even when you do research prior to the meeting?

- Recall the presentation in Hank's office when Abe neglected to discuss the product features and benefits. Why was Abe's *presentation* nevertheless effective?

Chapter 8

- Abe advises Adam to help him *build rapport*, "Assume you don't golf the next time your client talks about his golf game." What benefit is there to Adam to heed this advice?

- What is the significance of Adam struggling with his *understanding* (i.e., listening) skills even though he has once seen Abe do it so successfully?

- How did Adam behave in a typical, immature fashion when he pushed for a sale with the job superintendent? Describe ways in which this portrays reality.

- Comment on the differences between the presentations from Adam and Abe. In what ways is Abe's non-product *presentation* more effective than Adam's product "push"?
- Discuss a personal buying experience during which you learned about selling from the customer perspective. How can you apply the lesson to your selling skills?

Chapter 9

- Why does the writer go directly to the review of the sales call with Fred Deardon (rather than letting you see the actual call)? What does it tell you about the power of reviewing your own performance?
- Abe illustrates repeatedly the difference between good performances versus bad, regardless of the quality of the sales outcome. What does he mean by this? How valuable is this distinction?
- Adam describes the benefit his product will provide as a marketing asset to Fred Deardon. How is his *presentation*, although nearly identical to Abe's presentation to Hank Piquell, inappropriate under the circumstances?
- How is the dialogue between Abe and Adam evolving to become "peer to peer"? How does it differentiate from the dialogues between Adam and Joe?

Chapter 10

- Abe has finally revealed his full Non-Linear Sales Formula. What strikes you as realistic? How can this visual depiction of the process help you achieve more sales momentum with clients?
- What does Mary's observation of Adam's cockiness foreshadow? How does a lack of self-criticism in salespeople lead to the poor performances in reality?
- Why is Adam's horrible day in front of Abe so important to the story? If Abe had not observed Adam's poor performance, what do you expect it would have meant for Adam's future?
- What would you say about Abe's reaction to Adam's poor performance? Why is Abe happy with Adam as a performer in spite of his failure during the day?
- What does it mean that Abe calls sales leads "gems"?
- Is it realistic that an expected sale (with Fred Deardon) never came to fruition while an unexpected sale (with Hank Piquell) did? Discuss situations in which you expected a sale that fell through and another that came to fruition when you least expected it.

Chapter 11

- What is the sales secret?

- How does Abe help Adam establish credibility as a salesperson in the call with Bob Renquist?
- What does the interaction between Bob, Adam, Abe, and eventually Paul LaFontaine say about sales credibility and leadership?
- At one point, Abe asserts that asking a walk-in client to a retail store "Can I help you?" is just as bad as asking a client in a business-to-business situation "What else can I do for you?" What does he mean by this?
- Abe lists several reasons for creating future sales calls with Bob Renquist that Adam does not see. Abe asks Adam, "Are you looking [for them]?" What is the power of this question? What does it teach Adam about creating productive reasons for a sales call?
- When Adam suggests that Abe "didn't think for a second about those great questions," Abe assures him that he thought about them "at great length." What lessons can you take from that dialogue? What does this say about the difference between wisdom and knowledge?

Chapter 12

- What is Mary's purpose to the story?
- How does she help Adam grow?
- How does the conclusion illustrate the powerful difference between a transactional sales mindset and a relationship mindset?

- What are the ultimate conclusions one can make about the profession of selling as potentially honorable? What are the big picture responsibilities of being a salesperson?
- How did Adam finally fulfill his desire to achieve internal confidence and overcome his attachment to material gain? What "gains" did he achieve as a result of the process?
- Where do you think Adam evolves from here?

About the Author

Rick Davis is President of Building Leaders, a Chicago-based sales training company established in 1999, with the intention of delivering a commonsense message that would create powerful sales results. Over 25,000 business professionals have attended Rick's seminars in 42 states and 6 provinces.

Rick's body of work includes a decade of articles printed in over 20 publications. Rick is the contributing editor to *ProSales Magazine* where his regular sales advice column has won awards from The American Society of Business Publication Editors, most recently a Gold Medal for his profile on sales excellence. In addition, Rick's body of published work includes a decade of articles in over 20 publications; he also authored the book *Strategic Sales in the Building Industry*.

Rick's professional journey began with studies in Economics, Mathematics, Computers and Acting at the University of Michigan. Today, he resides in Chicago, Illinois where he balances his time between work, exercise, family, and his hobbies. He is a loving husband of sixteen years, an accomplished pianist, a gourmet cook, and enjoys a good session of Texas hold 'em poker. When he isn't reading a book on psychology, politics, history, or science, there is a good chance you'll see him keeping his mind sharp with a good television cartoon.

To book Rick as a speaker for your next event or to learn more about sales and sales management training programs for your company, visit www.buildingleaders.com